Seasons of
peace

REFLECTIONS & ACTIVITIES
ON PEACE WITH JUSTICE
FOR FAMILIES
—— & ——
SMALL GROUPS

Compiled by

BETH A. RICHARDSON

BASED ON SELECTED READINGS
FROM THE NEW COMMON LECTIONARY

The Upper Room
Nashville, Tennessee

Seasons of Peace

Scripture quotations designated RSV are from the Revised Standard Version of the Bible, copyrighted 1946, 1952, and © 1971 by the Division of Christian Education, National Council of the Churches of Christ in the United States of America, and are used by permission.

Scripture quotations designated NEB are from the *New English Bible*, © The Delegates of Oxford University Press and the Syndics of the Cambridge University Press 1961 and 1970, and are reprinted by permission.

Scripture quotations designated TEV are from the *Good News Bible, the Bible in Today's Version*, copyrighted by American Bible Society 1966, 1971, © 1976, and are used by permission.

"Song for Sadako," words by Villanova Students, music by Mary Lu Walker, is copyright 1985 by Mary Lu Walker, 16 Brown Road, Corning, New York, 14830, and is used by permission.

Excerpt from *Race and the Renewal of the Church* by Will D. Campbell is copyright © 1961 by W. L. Jenkins, The Westminster Press. Used by permission.

Poem from *Psalms of a Black Mother* by Theresa Greenwood, copyright 1970 by Werner Press, Inc., Anderson, Indiana, is used by permission.

Material from *The Twelve Prophets* is reprinted by permission of Soncino Press, London, N.Y.

Excerpt from *Cotton Patch Parables of Liberation* by Clarence Jordan and Bill Lane Doulos, published by Herald Press, is used by permission.

Material from *Living Toward a Vision* by Walter Brueggemann, published by United Church Press, is used by permission.

"Prayer for a Rescue Not Always Wanted" by Daniel H. Evans is used by permission of the author.

Excerpt from *With Head and Heart* by Howard Thurman, published by Harcourt Brace Jovanovich, Inc., is used by permission.

Excerpt from MY LIFE FOR THE POOR by Mother Teresa is adapted from p. 18 of that work. Copyright © 1985 by Jose Luis Gonzales Balado. Reprinted by permission of Harper & Row, Publishers, Inc.

Slightly adapted excerpt from A DOCTOR'S CASEBOOK IN THE LIGHT OF THE BIBLE by Paul Tournier is reprinted by permission of Harper & Row, Publishers, Inc. 1960.

"Pronouns" from *Burning Bush* by Karle Wilson Baker, published by Yale University Press, is copyright 1922, 1950 by Yale University Press and is used by permission.

Excerpt from sermon by Martin Luther King, Jr. is copyright © 1967 by Martin Luther King, Jr. and reprinted by permission of Joan Daves.

Excerpt from *The New Being* is copyright 1955 Paul Tillich; copyright renewed © 1983 Hannah Tillich. Reprinted with the permission of Charles Scribner's Sons.

Excerpt from *Ten Rungs: Hasidic Sayings* by Martin Buber is used by permission.

Book and Cover Design: Thelma Whitworth
First Printing: June 1986 (5)
Library of Congress Catalog Card Number: 86-50289
ISBN: 0-8358-0548-4
Printed in the United States of America

Contents

—————————— ■ ——————————

Preface

————————■————————

The Bible is saturated with concern for *shalom*. *Shalom* is a Hebrew word. We have adopted it into English, along with its meaning of peace that is more than merely the absence of war, peace that is instead a total, just, well-being. The cries of the poor, the oppressed, the outcast echo through the pages of the Bible. It is strange that people with a passion for peace and justice have so often neglected its supportive treasures. It is stranger yet that those who profess the Bible as their authority have so often ignored its teaching of shalom.

In *Seasons of Peace*, a group of concerned persons share their reflections on key Bible passages that relate to shalom. These reflections, while appropriate for use at any time, are arranged according to the days and seasons of the Christian year and the placement of passages in the Common Lectionary. Not only does use of the lectionary provide coverage of the Bible over the three-year cycle, it also sets before us, in every season of the year, the biblical call for shalom.

Countless other Bible passages can provide the basis for similar reflections. It is our hope that this resource will lead the reader to read and reflect more widely in the Bible itself through the perspective of shalom.

Hoyt Hickman

Introduction

—————————■—————————

Seasons of Peace is a resource to teach us how to live lives of peace with justice. It is intended to be used by small groups, families, individuals, or any others who want to live in shalom in the world.

Each section of *Seasons of Peace* contains a scripture reference and excerpt, a meditation, a prayer, hymn suggestions, a thought for reflection, and activities that relate to the scripture and Christian season. Reflections on the scripture and some of the prayers have been written by leaders committed to peace with justice, from diverse backgrounds and denominations.

This resource can be used in a variety of ways. Persons who use the book should feel the freedom to adapt the resource to meet their needs. Following are some possible uses for *Seasons of Peace.*

Small groups

Seasons of Peace may be used by small groups, such as prayer or study groups, gatherings of people around social issues, women's or men's church groups, and youth groups. If you are concerned about issues of peace with justice, use this book to focus the formation of a "covenant group" that works to increase awareness of peace with justice.

Read the meditation accompanying the scripture as a devotional for a meeting. Use the prayers in group worship experiences. Use *Seasons of Peace* as the focal point of a study on peace with justice. Read sections of the book for reflection together during meeting times. Adapt activities for the needs of your particular group and participate in them together.

If your group has a regular meeting space, create a worship center that will include symbols of worship that are meaningful to you. This center may include a candle, a Bible, or a map or globe of the world. If your group does not have a regular meeting place, choose symbols that you can bring to each meeting. These symbols can represent the bond of your group even as you are dispersed between your meetings.

Individuals

Seasons of Peace is appropriate for use by individuals as a resource for devotional life. Consider using the activities for your daily actions of faith. Keep a journal of your reflections on peace with justice, your learnings and your growth from participating in activities.

Choose a place that is your "worship center." It may be a particular chair or table or corner. Keep in this place your devotional materials—your Bible, meditation books, journal, a candle, or whatever you use in your life of reflection and prayer. Follow the suggestions of symbols to use during the various seasons of the Christian year.

Families

Families may use the book in their family worship and choose actions of faith appropriate for their family. For use with families that include small children, the following suggestions may be helpful:

1. Family worship should fit your family. Family worship time may or may not look like the organized worship in which your family normally participates. Worship is the act of paying divine honors to God. It may include the traditional methods of prayer, proclaiming, and singing; *or* it may take other forms such as discussion, service, creative activities, or quiet time.

Experiment with a variety of worship forms. See which forms work best for your family. Try a series of worship services using the pattern: sing, talk, pray. Try a ritual which includes praise, confession, the word or message, and offering or recommitment. Use the structure that feels most natural for your family.

2. Utilize family times that you already have. As you plan worship time for your family, think of the times that you are together. These would be natural times to gather for worship: mealtimes, the time just before going to bed, family meetings, family time on the weekends.

Build upon the ritual that is already included in your lives. If you usually say a grace before eating, include a simple ritual during this time. If your family often discusses happenings at church during the meal following worship, use this time to talk about how to apply the message to your lives.

3. Observe special events as occasions for family worship. Celebrate a new job, a good report card, a life passage. Have a service of remembrance at the time of a death or tragedy. Create a special ritual which is always used for birthdays.

4. Include children in the planning. Take care not to come into the experience with set ideas of what worship involves. Be open to whatever ideas children may bring. A worship experience may include a mealtime

discussion about an injustice in your local community; it may consist of singing a song which a child learned in church school. Do not be afraid to repeat concepts for younger children. And include a chance for the children to say what they think.

5. Make worship as visual and concrete as possible. When discussing another country, have a map or a globe to show where the country is. Use crafts, games, Bible stories, singing, talking, or guided meditation to illustrate the concepts. Take a "field trip" to a place in the community for which you are concerned or to which you are giving money.

6. Use symbols for worship. Include symbols such as candles, a cross, flowers, an Advent wreath. Or make up your own symbols. Arrange a centerpiece of flowers each time a birthday is celebrated. Burn a special candle when someone in the family has a difficult test, an important meeting, or is in need of special energy and prayer. Have a worship center where you keep your family's worship symbols.

7. Move slowly into family worship. If your family has not previously had a time of worship, move into it at a comfortable pace. Begin by having family observances of Advent and Lent. If those occasions go well, expand to other seasonal worship times.

8. Have fun together! Family worship can bring both challenging and special moments to your lives. Do not worry if the time, right now, is not right for your family. Remain open to those times when worship is the thing that your family needs. Live in praise to God!

Using the Lectionary

This book is based on selected readings from the New Common Lectionary. There are an average of two readings for each month of the Christian calender. The New Common Lectionary has a cycle of three years, and these twenty-four readings are taken from throughout that cycle. Persons may follow the readings as they appear in the lectionary, or they may use the scriptures independent of their place in the Christian year.

A lectionary is a tool developed to assist in the study and reading of the entire Bible. It lists a different set of readings for each Sunday of the year. The lectionary cycle is begun again at the end of each period of three years. You can find out which year of the cycle (A, B, or C) is current by checking with your local congregation or denomination.

The lectionary listings in this book occur in two ways. During the first half of the Christian year (Advent through Pentecost Sunday) the reading is listed by the particular Sunday in the church season and the year (Fourth Sunday of Lent, Year C). After the beginning of Pentecost, the readings are listed by the date of the Sunday and the lectionary year (Sunday between August 14 and 20, Year A).

Inclusiveness

It is the intention of *Seasons of Peace* to model inclusiveness as a necessary part of living in peace with justice. Inclusiveness of language, culture, lifestyle, and image remind us that no one part of the family of God has exclusive access to God. We are one body, many parts.

Living in the human world, however, brings us human limitations, and we are unable to be truly inclusive in all our endeavors. To be true to copyright agreements, we have quoted scripture texts accurately. These quotations are not always inclusive. We hope that these few instances do not block for you the message of those texts. And we wait with hope for more widely accepted inclusive translations of our biblical resources.

I gratefully acknowledge the work of the committee out of which the idea for this resource grew. Charla Honea, Hoyt Hickman, Sandy Hodge, and Bob Dungy have each left their special mark on *Seasons of Peace*.

May you journey well, in peace and in justice.

Beth A. Richardson

Observance of Advent

Advent, the four weeks before Christmas, is the time of preparation for the birth of Christ. The word *Advent* means "to come." During the season of Advent, we are preparing our hearts and our homes for Christ's coming. Jesus is not yet here! We are waiting and anticipating the celebration, but we are in a time of "not yet." During Advent, focus your mind and spirit on what has to be done before all is ready for Christ's coming.

1. Prepare our hearts: Use an Advent wreath and daily Advent devotional booklet (available from your local church or denomination) in your worship life.
2. Prepare our homes: Talk about the ways you can celebrate that are consistent with your understanding of the meaning of Jesus' birth. How will you decorate? What do presents mean? What kind of presents should you give? Give gifts that are "for Jesus," gifts that are for where Jesus is in the world. (Give a percentage of money spent for gifts to a special hunger project. Or give gifts that symbolize the meaning of Jesus' coming: a flock of ducks or a cow through the Heifer Project.)
3. Prepare our places of worship: Evaluate the celebrations you traditionally hold during Advent. Do they reflect an atmosphere of anticipation and preparation? What events or observances do you need to modify? How can you reflect in your decorations the values which you celebrate in Jesus' birth?

The Precondition of Peace

Kentucky

ISAIAH 2:1–5
FIRST SUNDAY OF ADVENT, YEAR A

[God] shall judge between the nations,
  and shall decide for many peoples;
and they shall beat their swords into plowshares,
  and their spears into pruning hooks;
nation shall not lift up sword against nation,
  neither shall they learn war any more.
                    —ISAIAH 2:4, RSV

The promise of peace held out in verse 4 of this passage so fascinates us that, in one form or another, we invoke this vision—so tantalizing and yet so intangible—again and again. Thanks to the Ploughshares organization, I wear a constant emblem of verse 4, a miniature sword being turned into a plowshare.

The focus of this passage, however, is not on the promise so much as on its precondition. Before peace can become a reality, the law, God's revealed will, the word of the Lord, must go forth from the City of God. Human beings have to learn the ways of God—the ways of goodness and justice.

Is this not where the problem comes to focus in our age and culture? Our civilization no longer has a temple that will draw all nations to learn from the Lord, to learn how human beings should act toward one another. Has it not been replaced by another kind of temple and another kind of worship? We place our confidence in human science and technology, while neglecting divine wisdom.

As Thomas Merton observed so keenly, human beings have "an instinctive need for harmony and peace, for tranquility, order and meaning." But Western technological society denies us precisely these things. It leaves us no place to seek truth for its own sake, no place to seek the Ground of Being, where these qualities can become reality. Autonomous science and technology, under no subordination to something higher—humanity, reason, God—have dehumanized and depersonalized humanity even as they have sought to aid it.

Those of us who so earnestly long for peace, therefore, must hear first Isaiah's summons to "go up to the mountain of the Lord, to the house of

14

the God of Jacob; that he may teach us his ways and that we may walk in his paths" (Isa. 2:3, RSV). The point of the precondition is that no matter how brilliant we are, we cannot really learn God's ways on our own. God's instructions penetrate to the very joints and marrow of our being. God alone can shape our character so that we instinctively do what is right.

In the parable of kingdom righteousness in Matthew 25:31–46, those invited to enter God's kingdom are persons who feed the hungry, give drink to the thirsty, clothe the naked, welcome strangers, and visit the sick and prisoners without even thinking about it. They are the God-taught. They embody the precondition for peace.

Prayer (Divide people into two sides, each side reading its respective part.)

Left: Come, let us go up to the mountain of the Lord, to the house of the God of Jacob;

Right: that he may teach us his ways and that we may walk in his paths.

Left: For out of Zion shall go forth the law, and the word of the Lord from Jerusalem.

Right: He shall judge between the nations, and shall decide for many peoples;

Left: and they shall beat their swords into plowshares, and their spears into pruning hooks;

Right: nation shall not lift up sword against nation, neither shall they learn war any more.

—Isaiah 2:3–4, RSV

Hymn Suggestions

"O Come, O Come, Emmanual"
"Hail to the Lord's Anointed"
"Come, Thou Long-Expected Jesus"

For Your Thoughts . . .

World peace, freedom, justice for all [humankind] are not achieved by apathetic, indifferent Christians. Conflicts in ideology are not resolved by failure to face controversial issues. . . . The kingdom of God becomes real when Christians live according to the power that worketh in us, demonstrating God's purpose for us all.—*Thelma Stephens*[1]

Action and Reflection

1. How would the world be different if all the swords were turned into plowshares and the spears into pruning hooks?

2. Think of an activity to do that will help turn a sword into a plowshare. Here are some examples:

15

Raise the money it would take to buy one gun. Donate that money to a peace group or a group that teaches third world countries how to grow food.

Decide not to ask for or buy any toys which promote the acceptance of war.

3. Make a symbol of a plowshare or pruning hook out of construction paper, wood, or other material. Put it in your worship space during Advent or use it as a decoration. Let it remind you of the ways that you can be turning swords into plowshares.

A Visitation

Martha Whitmore Hickman
Tennessee

LUKE 1:39–55
FOURTH SUNDAY OF ADVENT, YEAR C

> *And Mary said,*
> *"My soul magnifies the Lord,*
> *and my spirit rejoices in God my Savior,*
> *for he has regarded the low estate of his handmaiden.*
> *For behold, henceforth all generations will call me blessed."*
> —LUKE 1:46–48, RSV

It is a familiar story. This young woman, Mary—a teenager, frightened, still reeling from the encounter with the angel (who would believe her? had she been dreaming? was it some kind of crazy hallucination?)—becomes, suddenly, empowered. Not only is she empowered to believe she is to give birth to the son of God, but she claims that fact with pride and utter self-confidence! (Her confidence may have wavered in ensuing months. How glad she must have been to see the shepherds and the Wise Men—another sign this was indeed a marvelous child!)

But she is not just empowered to believe God has chosen her in her "low estate." She goes on to make pronouncements about God's disposition toward *all* the poor and lowly. She makes strong statements about God's justice in taking food and power and wealth from those who have more and giving them instead to those who have less.

How did she get this way—this simple peasant girl, young, suddenly pregnant out of wedlock? She had no claim that we know of to special wisdom and power.

No claim other than that the angel came! A visitation from God—whatever its message—brings its recipient power.

But she needs to check it out. Advised by the angel that her cousin Elizabeth is also pregnant, Mary goes to Elizabeth—probably looking for confirmation that what she thought she had experienced could really be so. We can imagine her phrasing the question as she goes . . . "Elizabeth, do you think I'm crazy?"

And when she gets there, Elizabeth feels her own baby leap in recognition. She and Mary, absolutely confirmed now, share their wonder and delight, their shared conviction that what was spoken to Mary by the angel is true.

But the story doesn't stop there—in a sort of private celebration of prospective mothers. In her new power and elation, Mary goes on to extend the ramifications of her story to *all* of low degree. Like a prophet, she proclaims God's power and justice—which will later be at the heart of Jesus' call for justice.

As we contemplate our own struggles for faith, justice, and peace, it is well to be reminded that visitations from God are not matters for private rejoicing only. They lay their claim upon us for corroboration and for nurture. First, perhaps, we will share them with a trusted other or a community. And then we will see that God's messages have a wider social claim upon us, that, in the power of the Most High, we may be agents of peace and justice in the life of the world.

Prayer

O God, as we await your advent during this season, we remember Mary who waited for the birth of a child. Like Mary, we will be visited with the message of hope, of justice, of love that your child brings. Prepare us for the coming of this message, that we may rejoice and proclaim the good news for all of low degree. We await your coming. Amen.

Hymn Suggestions

Any setting of the Magnificat (Mary's Song in Luke 1:46b–55)
"O Little Town of Bethlehem"
"What Child Is This?"
"Hark! the Herald Angels Sing"

For Your Thoughts . . .

Mary's submission to the will of God is in no way the abject submission of a slave who has no choice. On the contrary, it is the creative submission of the fully liberated being who is free to serve God.

—*Marianne Katoppo*[2]

Action and Reflection

1. Read slowly through the scripture and/or meditation. As you hear these words, what feelings and thoughts do you have about Mary's situation?

2. Think about what it would be like to be "of low degree" (poor) and pregnant and to have God tell you that your baby is going to be important to the world. What are Mary's thoughts and feelings?

3. What is the message of verses 46–55? (This is called the Magnificat because it is Mary's hymn to magnify God.)

Unto Us a Child Is Born

Abel T. Muzorewa
Harare, Zimbabwe

ISAIAH 9:2–7
CHRISTMAS EVE OR DAY, YEARS A, B, OR C

Of the increase of his government and of peace
there will be no end,
upon the throne of David and over his kingdom,
to establish it, and to uphold it
with justice and with righteousness
from this time forth and for evermore.
The zeal of the Lord of hosts will do this.

—ISAIAH 9:7, RSV

The South African government, and those who support it, believe that apartheid is the best way of creating and maintaining peace. For over 333 years, when blacks of South Africa were quiet and reconciled to the oppressive system, it was considered that there was peace. And when, today, women sit in quiet desperation about equal rights with men, the male-dominated world thinks that there is peace. Whenever oppressed groups are quietly hurting under circumstances that would be untolerable to other people, then the establishment and its constituency think they have peace.

Is this peace? This kind of peace is like undetected cancer. The absence of a reaction to ill-treatment and injustice should never be regarded as peace, because it can only be peace *without* justice.

Isaiah 9:2–7 deals primarily with a human condition infested with war and symbols of war. But there is a message of hope. A new king would overthrow the oppressor, dismantle the symbols of war, and establish an era of peace. Christians have adopted this message and have accepted Jesus as the One qualified to be mighty God and Prince of Peace.

Peace with justice is, therefore, possible on Jesus' terms only. True peace with justice can be ushered into our various habitats and circumstances only when we start with Jesus and take seriously the command, "You shall love your neighbor as yourself" (Matt. 22:39, RSV). We must learn to empathize daily with all people, realizing seriously and sincerely that God made all people of the world with one blood (Acts 17:26)—whether they are poor or rich, men or women, young or old, black, brown, yellow, red, or white. All are children of God who—especially today—hunger and thirst after peace with justice. All mothers, irrespective of social status, race, color, or creed suffer the same labor pain when they bring people of God into the world. These mothers feel the same pain and sorrow when their children are deprived of a peace with righteousness and justice.

On a personal level, peace with justice is tranquility and harmony of the soul. On a social level, peace with justice is the absence of humanly inflicted pain and the presence of an abundance of liberty based on love. The best way of creating and promoting peace is to truly and sincerely love people and to work hard to create a peace based on that love.

Let us ponder these questions honestly. How can we restore and maintain peace with justice in family, group, church, country, and the world? Have I been doing to and for others those things I wish people would do to and for me? How would I feel if my attitude and behavior toward others were directed toward me?

Prayer

Lord Jesus, you are the only true Prince of Peace. Please forgive us our lack of justice in the things we do or do not do in the name of peace. Fill us now with your true peace, which surpasses all understanding; and help us to overthrow the power of evil and darkness from the throne of our hearts. Empower us so that we may be true messengers and instruments of peace with justice. And let it begin with me and in my home. May our world accept Jesus' terms of peace with justice. Amen.

Hymn Suggestions

"Joy to the World!"
"It Came upon the Midnight Clear"
"O Come, All Ye Faithful"

For Your Thoughts . . .

The pressing problem is not how to devise abstract models of a just society but how to effect the transition from less to more human relationships within our given situation.—*Peter Matheson*[3]

Action and Reflection

1. Welcome the Christ Child! Light the Christ candle if you have had an Advent wreath. Sing your favorite Christmas carols. Act out the Christmas story.

2. Remember the people, countries, communities that you have talked about, studied, prayed for during the past several months. What are they doing today? Have a prayer for the human family today.

3. The celebration of Christmas continues for twelve days until Epiphany and the coming of the Wise Ones. Plan together an activity or observance for each day. Remember those who may be forgotten in the days *after* a special holiday: the hungry, the lonely, the sick, the prisoners, the homeless.

4. After plans have been made, sing "Go Tell It on the Mountain."

Observance of Epiphany

The word epiphany comes from a Greek word meaning to show forth or manifest. During Epiphany, we celebrate the manifestation of God in Jesus Christ. Epiphany begins on the twelfth day of Christmas with the visit of the Magi, the foreign ones, to the Christ child. It continues until the beginning of Lent.

During the season of Epiphany, we focus on such events as the coming of the Magi, Jesus' baptism, the call of Jesus as One who will bring justice, the calling of his disciples, and his work in the world. These events point to Jesus as a representative of the God of *all* people, the God who wishes shalom for all.

As you celebrate Epiphany, carry with you the sense that it is a time of beginnings. Christ is breaking into the darkness of the world, spreading the radical message of God's salvation. God's light shows forth into a world that has not seen the light. Let yourself reflect upon the wonder that must have filled those people who first heard Jesus' message of justice and hope.

Kingdom People

Dana Beth McGraw
Tennessee

LUKE 3:10–22
BAPTISM OF THE LORD, YEAR C

The people asked [John the Baptist], "Then what are we to do?" He replied, "The [one] with two shirts must share with [the one] who has none, and anyone who has food must do the same."

—LUKE 3:10–11, NEB

Everything about the message of John the Baptist is startling: the time is now; the kingdom of heaven is at hand! A Hebrew heritage is not enough; repent, be baptized, and live like kingdom people! John's hearers picked up dramatic prophetic echoes that have been largely lost to our contemporary ears.

A call to baptism sounds startling indeed to John's audience, who know nothing of a baptism rite except to initiate Gentile proselytes into the faith—a rather insulting comparison for a faithful Jew! And yet, John implies, entrance into the kingdom that is at hand is no less radical a change than going from Gentile to Jew.

John says that he baptizes with water, but that the One to come will baptize with the spirit and with fire, two familiar Hebrew Messianic images. In the words of the prophets, the God of justice, in the coming age, will pour out the Spirit of God on all people and will cause them to pass through the refiner's fire. What might it be like to be immersed in the very Spirit of God, to be dipped in fire? To the Jews of John the Baptist's time, these images signal that the anticipated reign of justice is being ushered in and that they must be prepared.

In the same way, the words spoken from heaven upon Jesus' baptism echo Isaiah's description of the Messiah (Isa. 42:1). The radical, almost blasphemous message of John is that these words are being fulfilled at the moment, in the One whose shoes he is not fit to untie.

Equally shocking to the people of that day is John's judgment on his audience: being children of Abraham is not enough! They must repent and bear fruit as evidence of their repentance. Their lives must be changed. The Hebrew sense of repentance is tied up in a directive to live in peace and justice; the wicked must mend their ways to do what is just and right. To John this means specifically that the person with two shirts must share with someone who has none, and anyone with food must do the same. Justice demands that all live simply, sharing the earth's goods.

John's message is remarkable, but the response of the people is more remarkable still. They ask simply, "Then what are we to do?" They lived "on the tiptoe of expectation" (v. 15, NEB) looking for the Messiah.

Today, we live in a multilayered time in which the Epiphany is past, present, and future. The Christ has come; the kingdom is within us and among us still; we look toward the eschaton yet to come. In this time that some have called "between the ages," we must continue on the tiptoe of expectation. We must be startled by the message of radical obedience . . . so much so that we cannot but ask, "Then what are we to do to usher in an age of peace with justice?" We must live like kingdom people!

Prayer

Leader: God of fire and water, you call us to be kingdom people,
People: potters of justice and molders of peace.
Leader: As we celebrate Jesus' baptism for ministry,
People: we renew our special callings to God's work in the world.
Leader: We live on the tiptoe of expectation;
People: startle us with your message of renewal.
All: We pray, in Jesus' name. Amen.

Hymn Suggestions

"The Church's One Foundation"
"Jesus, the Sinner's Friend, to Thee"
"Come, Every Soul by Sin Oppressed"

For Your Thoughts . . .

Freedom will come when one is willing to restrain one's own freedom for the sake of others, and justice will come when those who are not hurt by injustice are as indignant as those who are.—*Joseph B. Fabry*[4]

Action and Reflection

1. Talk about ways that you or your family or group can fulfill a special calling. You might want to visit a lonely person in prison, help tutor in an after-school program for inner-city children, tell friends how much their friendship means to you.

2. Using paper or fabric, create a symbol of a dove to remind you of your special calling as a child of God. Make a small dove for each person to wear; or, make one large dove and place it in a prominant place in your home or place of worship.

3. Do the following liturgy together.

—Sing one of the hymns listed above.

—Share your calling or how you will help the family/group calling.

—Ritualize your reaffirmation of your baptism and your special calling by putting on or hanging your dove.

—Say the above prayer together.

And Hope Came . . .

Lee Ranck
Maryland

LUKE 4:14–21
THIRD SUNDAY AFTER EPIPHANY, YEAR C

Jesus said, *"The Spirit of the Lord is upon me,*
because he has anointed me to preach good news to the poor.
He has sent me to proclaim release to the captives
and recovering of sight to the blind,
to set at liberty those who are oppressed,
to proclaim the acceptable year of the Lord."
—LUKE 4:18–19, RSV

Publicity about the guest speaker for the World Order Sunday observance at Foremost United Methodist Church, Yourtown, had stirred widespread interest. That Sunday the congregation filled the sanctuary and overflowed into adjacent meeting rooms. The people had come to hear the young man who had grown from their congregation to become one of the country's most revered preachers. The eyes of all in the church were fixed on him as he stood in the pulpit to speak. And he opened the book of the prophet Isaiah and read:

"The Spirit of the Lord is upon me, because he has anointed me to preach good news to *you* poor. He has sent me to proclaim release to *you* captives, and recovering of sight to *you* blind, to set at liberty *you* who are oppressed, to proclaim *your* acceptable year of the Lord."

As he paused, the people looked questioningly at one another. The familiar passage, which their own minister often quoted, sounded different. Why had he said *"you* poor," *"you* captives," *"you* blind," *"you* who are oppressed"? Why had he revised the Scripture? Puzzled, disturbed, they waited for the preacher to continue.

"World order, peace with justice, begins right here with you. I bring good news to *you* poor—poor in spirit. In the midst of all that you have, saddled with affluence that has separated you from your neighbors who are physically poor, burdened with things that you have come to value more than your fellow human beings.

"I bring release to *you* captives—captives to profits, success, security, comfort, luxuries, technology so that too often you are unable to see and respond to the real captives in the world.

"I offer recovered sight to *you* blind—blind to the systems that have oppressed and repressed others while rewarding you; blind to the subtle racism, sexism, ageism, handicapism that has brought pain and discrimination to so many others; blind to the stream of need flooding past your protective dike around this magnificent church building.

"I will set *you* oppressed at liberty—oppressed by the need for more and more, by the crush to 'get ahead,' to obtain and hold fast to 'the good life.' I will set you free to experience the exhilaration of working to free and uplift others who live in the oppression of poverty, ignorance, and tyranny.

"I will proclaim *your* acceptable year of the Lord—when the thoughts and ideas of your minds and the labor of your bodies contribute to the present and coming Kingdom of God and become part of the assurance of justice in a world of peace."

When the guest preacher closed the book and sat down, some of the people grumbled uncomfortably to each other; others glared at him; and others shook their heads as if to clear the misunderstanding. But in the back pew a young woman smiled, though tears filled her eyes, as she looked at the face of the guest. Her name was Hope.

Prayer (Divide people into two sides, each side reading its respective part.)

Left: O God of all, in the poverty of our spirits we hear the good news Christ brought into the world.
Right: Release us captives from our restricting chains;
Left: open our eyes to the needs of justice surrounding us;
Right: break us into the freedom of loving, abundant living;
Left: use us in the quest for peace with justice
Right: until all your people live in that acceptable year of the Lord.
All: Amen.

Hymn Suggestions

"Love Divine, All Loves Excelling"
"Breathe on Me, Breath of God"
"O Spirit of the Living God"

For Your Thoughts . . .

The religion of Jesus offers a promising way to work through the conflicts of a disordered world. I make a careful distinction between Christianity and the religion of Jesus [which] projected a creative solution to the pressing problem of survival for the minority of which He was a part.
—*Howard Thurman*[5]

25

Action and Reflection

1. A modern-day prophet, teacher, and preacher was Martin Luther King, Jr. Talk about the similarities and differences that you see between this story and Martin Luther King's life.

2. Think of ways to celebrate the birthday of Martin Luther King, Jr. Check on local activities in which to participate. Learn and sing at your meals, "Free at Last," "Oh, Freedom," or "We Shall Overcome." Those who can remember, tell stories of the days when Dr. King lived and worked. Or read together a book about Dr. King's life (check with your church or public library for a biography of Martin Luther King).

Forgotten Covenant

Daniel H. Evans
Missouri

MICAH 6:1–8
FOURTH SUNDAY AFTER EPIPHANY, YEAR A

> [God] has showed you, O man, what is
> good;
> and what does the Lord require
> of you
> but to do justice, and to love
> kindness,
> and to walk humbly with your
> God?
>
> —MICAH 6:8, RSV

In this passage from Micah, the prophet is presenting the arguments of Yahweh against the people of Israel. Like a prosecutor arguing before a court, God accuses Israel of forgetting the covenant sealed by God's saving acts.

In the second section (6:6–7), the prophet lists the people's feeble defense. They ask, "What else do you want us to do?" Shall the people come with calves to burn or the offering of their firstborn or ten thousand rivers of oil or thousands of rams to sacrifice? No, the answer is simple: what the Lord requires is "to do justice, and to love kindness, and to walk humbly with your God."

Still today, God has a charge against us. We have forgotten our covenant. "We tithe and go to church! We even give to United Way! What more does God require?" Let us plead our case before the mountains and let the hills hear our voice. And let us do that which the Lord requires . . . to do justice and love kindness and walk humbly with our God.

Prayer for a Rescue Not Always Wanted

Save us
O generous and patient God of Jesus,
  not just from hardness of heart,
    but from thickness of head.
Deliver us from the paralyzing myopia
  that allows a vision no further distant
    than our own limited experience,
      parochial concerns,
        selfish fetishes.

27

Unleash us from the passions that seal off
   the touch of the neighbor or the
     passing stranger because that one
       lacks some list of artificial
         prerequisites: the color of
           skin, the size of the paycheck.
Lift from our minds the yoke
   of selfishness and greed,
     of small imagination and the demon sloth,
      of busyness in little things and
        narrow insight in the greater.
Unharness us from the self-imposed burdens
   of fashion in the guise of acceptance,
     of peer group pressure wearing the mask of
     wisdom, and
       the slavish worship of ways old
        or new.
Set us free
   in that mighty freedom of forgiving love,
     whose renewing devotion is
       respect for persons,
         reverence for life,
           honor of the truth, and
             hope for each becoming. Amen.[6]

Hymn Suggestions

  "O Master, Let Me Walk with Thee"
  "What Shall I Render to My God?"
  "O For a Closer Walk with God"
  "Just a Closer Walk with Thee"

For Your Thoughts . . .

Micah felt the deepest sympathy with the misery and destitution to which the rapaciousness of the rich and powerful had reduced the masses; but also he saw that a society built on tyranny, corrupted and false standards of wealth, was a society doomed to destruction.

—The Twelve Prophets[7]

Action and Reflection

  1. Micah was a prophet, one who speaks God's will. In the scripture, Micah is telling the people of Israel that God is displeased with them and that they must act differently in order to be good followers of God. Are there prophets today who remind us that we are not doing what God requires of us? Who are our prophets? What are they saying?

2. Is it possible for us to be prophets to each other? Make a covenant, a promise with your family, group, or community that you will speak the truth with each other. This truth should be spoken with love and with openness to hear what others have to say. (For example, a prophet might say, "I think we spend too much time watching television and not enough time learning about the community around us. What do you think?")

3. Have a ritual to acknowledge these promises. Read the prayer of confession above, then state the promises that you make to each other. (Such as: I will speak the truth in love; I will listen to what others have to say; I will look for the ways we do and do not walk in justice.)

Choose Life

John B. Cobb, Jr.
California

DEUTERONOMY 30:15–20
SIXTH SUNDAY AFTER EPIPHANY, YEAR A

Moses said, "I summon heaven and earth to witness against you this day: I offer you the choice of life or death, blessing or curse. Choose life and then you and your descendants will live."

—DEUTERONOMY 30:19, NEB

The puzzling thing about this passage is that it is not addressed to individuals, but to the whole people of Israel. It is Israel that will prosper or decay, live or die, according to obedience.

That is puzzling for us because we think of individuals as the only deciders. If my nation does what is right, that does not make me righteous. If my nation acts badly, that does not make me a sinner. I am judged according to my own choices within the limits set by larger social forces.

But Israel knew what we sometimes forget. We are so bound together with others that, even as individuals, we can escape neither the responsibility nor the consequences of our corporate acts. If our nation behaves pridefully, if it relies more on military force than on the appeal of democratic ideals, if it justifies actions on its side that it condemns in others, then we are all caught up in the guilt, and we all suffer the consequences.

Deuteronomy is not dealing primarily with international relations. The question of life and death has to do with the internal order of the society—family, property, the alien in the midst, the structure of power, even the treatment of animals. If society is well-ordered, it will be healthy and vital. But if those who have the power to order society ignore the rights of those who lack the power to defend themselves, justice gives way to tyranny, and the nation moves toward death.

Citizens of the United States have much to be proud of in this respect. Its rulers have been bound by a constitution that functions much as the Deuteronomic law was designed to function for Israel. Rarely have presidents transgressed these bounds. The army has accepted civilian rule and never seriously threatened it. Provisions have been made for the poor to insure that they do not fall into utter misery.

But on this last point, we are below Biblical standards, and the lot of the poor has grown worse. On one side, the economy renders more and more workers superfluous. On the other side, we hear more and more often that we cannot afford to continue the level of help we have been accustomed to giving to the unemployed and unemployable.

It is time to listen again, collectively as a people, to the Bible. Our destiny depends on whether we heed the word of God or the attraction of mammon. When we abandon our sisters and brothers to hunger and homelessness, death's icy hand begins its work. The hungry and home-less weaken and die physically. The insensitive affluent die spiritually. The nation dies morally first, and then, gradually, politically as well. Let us instead choose life.

Prayer

Oh God of Justice, we gratefully acknowledge your gift of justice. Draw now our hearts to you that we may live. Renew our commitment to your way. Check our greed and our arrogance. Strengthen our sisterly and brotherly concern for one another. Help us as a people to evaluate anew our human justice in relation to the ultimate justice which is your purpose for us. For we pray in the name of the One who came that we might have life and have it more abundantly. Amen.

Hymn Suggestions

"The Voice of God Is Calling"
"Where Cross the Crowded Ways of Life"
"God of Grace and God of Glory"

For Your Thoughts . . .

Ultimately, you must do right because it is right to do right. . . . You must be just because it is right to be just. . . . If you have never found something so dear and so precious to you that you will die for it, then you are unfit to live.—*Martin Luther King, Jr.*[8]

Action and Reflection

1. What are the ways that nations of the world choose death? Choose life? How does your country choose? Look through a newspaper and pick out examples of the ways we choose life and choose death.

2. Are there structures in our societies that are set up to help the powerless? What are they? Think of ways you can work to improve these structures.

3. This scripture passage is an example of the challenge that was tradi-tionally presented at the climax of ancient covenant renewal ceremonies. God is challenging us to choose between life and death. Renew your promises to God in this Covenant Renewal Liturgy.

31

—Symbols: Have a dead branch and a living flower or plant. The dead branch represents the death of turning away from God's commandments. The living flower or plant represents the life of loving and obeying God by seeking justice and peace.

—Litany of Confession: Call out words or phrases that suggest ways you or your country choose death instead of life.

—Litany of Covenant Renewal: Call out words or phrases that tell the ways you promise to choose life.

—Pray the prayer listed above.

Observance of Lent

———————■———————

Lent is the period of self-examination and penitence which precedes Easter. It begins on Ash Wednesday and ends in Easter, symbolizing Jesus' forty days in the wilderness. Lent has traditionally been observed with prayer, fasting, and almsgiving (see Matt. 6:1–18).

Choose ways to observe Lent as individuals, as families, or as a group. Have a simple meal of rice and beans once a week and donate the money that you save to a hunger project. Fast every Friday from noon to six o'clock to symbolize the six hours that Jesus was on the cross. Pick a place in your community or in the world that is in need of peacemaking. Daily or weekly, have a time of individual, group, or family prayer for this place. Think about situations close to you where peace is needed, and confess ways you have not been helpful and pray for wisdom to find ways to respond.

Called to Courage

Gwen White
New York

EXODUS 3:1–15
THIRD SUNDAY OF LENT, YEAR C

"Come now; I will send you to Pharaoh and you shall bring my people Israel out of Egypt." "But who am I," Moses said to God, "that I should go to Pharaoh, and that I should bring the Israelites out of Egypt?" God answered, "I am with you. This shall be the proof that it is I who have sent you: when you have brought the people out of Egypt, you shall all worship God here on this mountain."
—EXODUS 3:10–12, NEB

In the reading of these verses from Exodus, we discover an interesting sequence of movement between God and Moses.

• God does something to gain the attention of Moses.
• God speaks to Moses out of concern for a suffering and afflicted people.
• God makes a request of Moses to become involved, and chooses him to do a specific thing.
• Moses feels incompetent for the task and gives excuses why he is not capable for such a responsibility.
• God gives Moses assurance that he will not be alone in the task. God promises Presence with him in every situation that may arise.

This scenario sounds so familiar in our own time. What are the many ways in which God is constantly trying to get *our* attention, and make *us* aware of the suffering, injustice, and agony of peoples all over the world, beginning even in our own communities?

As a people of God, the request comes to us to become involved. If we listen closely to God's call in our lives, we may be given specific tasks which will require us to become messengers, confronters, reconcilers, consolers, peacemakers, and healers.

But, how often we become like Moses! The world seems so overwhelming and the task so great, that we'd rather find a hundred excuses why we are not the ones for the task. We are always certain there is someone else who can do it better than we.

However, God calls those who don't always feel up to the task. The real issue we must face is not God's call, but an obedient response to God on our part and empowerment *by* God to do what we are to do. God does not expect us to rely upon our own strength and resources alone. We are only asked to say "yes," to the nudging spirit that asks us to care for the creation and all the peoples of the world.

Moses' greatest fear was probably the same as our own; that of confronting those who seemingly hold power and control over masses of people.

Regardless of this, confrontation is essential. Situations must change. Systems must change. Perceptions of reality must change. We, like Moses, must find our voices of protest and move into the arenas of power with a courage that can only come through faith.

There is an anonymous saying, "Courage is fear which has said its prayers." Faithful people are praying people, finding courage, strength, and sustenance in a continuing dialogue with a relational God. This God is the same God who, as with Moses, promises empowerment, Presence, and results on behalf of peace and justice in this world.

Prayer

Leader: Loving God, here we are in your presence, standing upon holy ground, longing to hear you speak to us,

People: yet fearful of our own unworthiness and inadequacies before you.

Leader: Help us to discover and trust your enabling and empowering love for us.

People: Grant us the discernment, vision, and courage to know and do your will in our time.

Leader: Help us speak out for justice on behalf of others

People: and walk in the paths of peace toward the realization of your shalom in this, your world.

All: Amen.

Hymn Suggestions

"Praise to the Living God" ("The God of Abraham Praise")
"Go Down, Moses"
"Once to Every Man and Nation"

For Your Thoughts . . .

The suffering of man is also the suffering of God. That is always my reply to those who tell me that they can't believe in God in the face of all the suffering that goes on in the world. God is the greatest sufferer.

—*Paul Tournier*[9]

Action and Reflection

1. Act out the story of Moses and the burning bush. Have three people read the parts of God, Moses, and a narrator.

2. What were the feelings that Moses might have had during the experience with God? Have you ever had any of those feelings?

3. Have you ever had a time when you thought you couldn't do something? What happened? How can you help someone in a situation like this?

35

Opening Our Eyes

Liz Lopez Spence
New Mexico

JOHN 9:1–41
FOURTH SUNDAY OF LENT, YEAR A

With these words [Jesus] spat on the ground and made a paste with the spittle; he spread it on the man's eyes, and said to him, "Go and wash in the pool of Siloam." (The name means "sent.") The man went away and washed, and when he returned he could see.

—JOHN 9:6–7, NEB

For a period of time, I was living in Bolivia. Coming from a peaceful nation, the United States, the rude awakening to war in Bolivia was a transforming element in my life. Once I was at a parade with a friend. Suddenly there were soldiers, guns, tanks, tear gas. As my friend and I scrambled for safety, the "peace" I had always taken for granted at "home" took on new meaning. It became a gift. To experience danger to one's life in the face of war is a powerful symbol to one who experiences it for the first time. My eyes were opened to a new dimension of life, seeing anew the people who lived with war on a daily basis. A blindness in my life had been "healed." But with the healing came the challenge to struggle, for the rest of my life, with how I would act on this healing.

Like the blind man whose credibility of vision was tested after being healed by Jesus, the credibility of our visions of peace with justice stand at the forefront of our faith waiting to be tested, to be believed. As the blind man became an agent of the power of God, it is apparent that he was never abandoned by God. This affirmation says the same to us, that God never abandons us to the forces of unbelief, sin, and injustice, but calls us to become agents of hope to empower those who share our visions of a just world of peace.

The challenge of the blind man calls us to allow Jesus to open our eyes and to act on our healing, keeping our eyes open to the realities of peace, justice, life, faith, and hope. The challenge of the blind man calls us to do what it takes to accomplish these realities and to be willing to go before our neighbors, parents, religious leaders, congregations and say, "Yes, I can see," and, ultimately, "Yes, Christ, I believe, make me an instrument of your peace."

Peacemaking is not an optional commitment. It is a requirement of faith by the Christ who rubs our eyes with his call to a new life of peace;

36

who heals the blindness that prevents us from living in a world of wholeness (shalom), a state of harmony with God, humanity, and all creation.

It is in the blind man that God's power and works have been manifested. It is in you and me that God's power and works are manifested. And it is through us that this world can be transformed into a world of peace with justice.

Our eyes have been opened! Let us join the journey of peace! Let us walk the road of shalom!

Prayer

Christ, who rubs our eyes with the call to a new life, heal the blindness that prevents us from living in a world of wholeness. Transform our hearts as well as our eyes, that we may join your journey of peace, justice, and shalom. Amen.

Hymn Suggestions

"Amazing Grace"
"Open My Eyes That I May See"
"O For a Thousand Tongues to Sing"

For Your Thoughts . . .

Do not tell yourself that you are greater than your neighbor, because you serve God so very fervently. You are no different from the rest of the creatures who were created for the service of God. —*Martin Buber*[10]

Action and Reflection

1. a. Have you ever had an experience when you felt your eyes had been opened to a new reality? Describe the experience. How did you feel? What were the reactions of other people to your experience?
b. What do you think happened later to the man who had been healed? Did his life change? How? Was your life changed with your experience? Are there things that you need to see again in a new way?

2. Do you know people who are physically challenged (who are blind, deaf, in a wheelchair)? What ways are you the same or different from them? The next time you are together, talk about your similarities.

37

Signs of Victory

Beth A. Richardson
Tennessee

MARK 15:1–39
PASSION/PALM SUNDAY, YEAR B

And when the centurion, who stood facing him, saw that he thus breathed his last, he said, "Truly this man was the Son of God!"
—MARK 15:39, RSV

Betrayal, darkness, mockery . . . not the expected ending to the glorious entry into Jerusalem, the climax of life and career of the Messiah. The scripture tells the bitter story of Jesus' trial, conviction, humiliation, and public execution. It is a story of fear and defeat, of pain and death.

We read the story already knowing the ending: God's victory. But Easter is not here yet, and Passion week calls us to reflect on the experience of defeat, of disappointment, of disbelief. Most of us can, in some ways, identify with the feelings of those followers of Jesus who witnessed the destruction of hope and belief with the death of their teacher.

We see, not believing, the events before us. We recall vivid memories of the deaths of such leaders of hope as Gandhi, John F. Kennedy, and Martin Luther King. How much more final must Jesus' death have seemed. If his teachings were true, then why this public rejection? Why is he not performing a miracle to save himself? Could his miracles, his teachings have been illusion? If all we believed was true, how could this be happening?

We withdraw from others around us in shock, in horror, in confusion. We face the darkness alone, unsure of what is safe to say or do or believe. Our hopes for peace have been dashed. We watch from afar for the moment that God's angels will come and save him. But they do not come. And Jesus dies a painful death surrounded by criminals, mocking guards, gawking crowds, and silent followers.

In the midst of the darkness, however, there are signs that point toward the victory. At the moment of Jesus' death, the curtain of the Temple is torn in two, a sign of God's grief. Those standing near a centurion hear him utter a confession, "Surely this man was the Son of God." One who knew not becomes a believer. Witnesses of darkness feel the power of God in the midst of despair.

38

We look for signs of God's victory in our lives. World leaders decide to talk about peace even as they continue to build armaments. The memory of a loved one comforts us as we grieve their death. Faithful people quietly work for justice in the slums and barrios of the world.

What will be the outcome? For the crucifixion: Resurrection. For the darkness in our lives, the threat of nuclear war, the hopelessness of famine, the meaningless destruction of our delicate world balance: we do not know. We can only trust in the faithfulness of God, looking for signs that point through the darkness toward the victory.

Prayer

God of Jesus, we remember with grief the crucifixion of Jesus, your son. The story reminds us that you are with us in our times of defeat and despair. Give us awareness to see the signs of your victory in the midst of the darkness in our lives. We await your victory. Amen.

Hymn Suggestions

"O Young and Fearless Prophet"
"Were You There"

For Your Thoughts . . .

By choosing the way of the cross, resisting people with goodness, moral weakness with spiritual strength, Christ sought not a life of indulgence and personal glory for himself but a way of salvation and enlightenment for all humankind. —*Aly Wassil*[11]

Action and Reflection

1. What are signs that point toward God's victory in the midst of darkness and death? List the signs on a sheet of paper and keep it in your worship space during Holy Week, the week before Easter.

2. Plant seeds or bulbs as a sign of God's transformation of death into life. (Plant seeds or bulbs outside, if possible, or inside in cups or pots if the season is not right.)

3. In your worship space, use symbols which remind you of the sadness and confusion of the events that are observed this week. If you have a cross, drape it with black cloth. Leave your worship candle unlit until Easter morning. Decorate your table with a dry branch.

Observance of Easter

—■—

The season of Easter begins with the celebration of the Resurrection of Christ on Easter morning. The mourning period is over. Jesus has broken the bonds of death and the message for all of us is life!

During the season of Easter, the scripture readings tell the story of Jesus' disciples spreading the word that Christ has brought forgiveness and freedom. The work begins to interpret the meaning of the resurrection.

During this season of the Christian year, when celebration is certainly appropriate, we must be careful to remember that Easter means beginnings. The celebration does not end with inactivity. It ends with people going out to live and tell the good news of the risen Christ. As you celebrate this Easter season, reflect on the question: Who are the people who need to hear and see the good news?

Acting on the Resurrection

Beth A. Richardson
Tennessee

ACTS 5:17–32
SECOND SUNDAY AFTER EASTER, YEAR C

The high priest questioned them, saying, "We strictly charged you not to teach in this name, yet here you have filled Jerusalem with your teaching." . . . But Peter and the apostles answered, "We must obey God rather than men."
—ACTS 5:27–29, RSV

The Resurrection brings transformation. Jesus is raised from the dead and life is transformed. The apostles spread the message that a new covenant has been given by God. God wishes life for all God's children . . . Jews and Gentiles, slave and free, male and female.

The Resurrection transforms the disciples. Are these the followers who denied knowing Jesus, who dispersed in silence and shame when Jesus was arrested and crucified? In the scripture passage, we find these same disciples preaching Christ's message without thought of government restrictions or their personal safety.

Acts 5:17–32 tells the story of the arrest of the apostles by the high priest and Sadducees. An angel releases them from jail, allowing the apostles to return to their preaching in the temple. When they are brought before the high priest a second time, Peter and the apostles must answer the priest's question, "Why did you disobey?" Their answer: "We must obey God rather than men."

The apostles were compelled to preach Christ's message even to the point of disobedience of human authorities. This "divine obedience" was a characteristic of the early Christian movement. Followers of Jesus broke both civil and Jewish laws and faced severe punishment for this.

They preached the message that the old laws are transformed to a new way of being. They preached that Jews and Gentiles may eat and worship together, that there is freedom for all. Slaves and women, for the first time, carried responsibility for sharing the good news. Christian men refused to serve in the army because of Jesus' call for love.

Today, we see that such willingness to follow God's commands was a brave act of faith. During their day, the early Christians were looked upon as radical fanatics, fools, criminals.

Since the days of the early Christians, Christ's followers have been transformed by the Resurrection. Many of these followers have felt called to "divine obedience" as they have refused military service, have preached freedom for all, or have acted as they believed they were called to act. During the period of slavery in the United States, some Christians felt called to assist slaves to freedom on the Underground Railroad. Today, sanctuary workers risk prosecution to help those they believe are political refugees. Peace advocates witness against nuclear arms and military buildup by performing acts that lead to their arrest.

These acts are often misunderstood and rejected by the status quo and civil authorities. But these acts are statements of faith by people who believe that God has called them to obey a higher authority.

God calls each of us to live in "divine obedience." Each of our callings is personal and individual, as we are called to different tasks. Let us be open to God's calling. Let us strive to obey a higher authority in whatever way is right for us. Let us continue to spread the good news. Let us be transformed by the Resurrection.

Prayer

Leader: You call us, O God, to be followers of Jesus.

People: Help us live in "divine obedience" to you.

Leader: As we celebrate the Resurrection, let us be aware of your special tasks for us.

People: Enable us to live the good news with love and enthusiasm.

Leader: Christ is risen!

People: We are transformed!

Hymn Suggestions

"Hope of the World"

"I Would Be True"

For Your Thoughts . . .

Isn't it time for somebody to get up and say, . . . "We are not going into mass exchanges of nuclear weapons." And who should refuse to drink from the giant vats of the Pentagon, if not those who take the cup of salvation from their Lord and Savior!—*William Sloane Coffin, Jr.*[12]

Action and Reflection

1. What is the message of the good news? Talk about the special message that the apostles preached to those who would listen. What was special about the message?

2. Have you ever had a belief that was so strong that you disobeyed laws or rules in order to follow it? What was that belief? What other beliefs would cause you to disobey human authorities?

3. During your meditation time this week, read writings by Gandhi or Martin Luther King. Each of these people risked his life for beliefs that he held. (Check your community or church library for writings by these persons.)

Observance of Pentecost

───────■───────

Pentecost is, for Christians, the birth of the church. The event of the coming of the Holy Spirit occurred on the Day of Pentecost (the fiftieth day after Passover), the day, held by Jewish tradition, on which the law was given. On that first Day of Pentecost after the Resurrection, there were many pilgrims in Jerusalem who had come for the celebration. These pilgrims were on hand to witness the birth of the Christian church and to experience firsthand the coming of the Holy Spirit as it proclaimed the message of the Christ in each persons' own language.

The season of Pentecost lasts for the rest of the Christian year, until the beginning of Advent. Pentecost recalls the beginning of the work of the church and the beginning of our work as people of faith.

With the gift of the fire of the Holy Spirit, we are equipped to do God's work in God's world. During the season of Pentecost, the liturgical color red reminds us of the work for justice to be done. We spread the word of God's shalom through our lives, that each person may "hear" God's message in their own "language."

The Family of God

H. B. Cavalcanti
Pernambuco, Brazil

ACTS 2:1-21
PENTECOST, YEARS A, B, OR C

Now there were living in Jerusalem devout Jews drawn from every nation under heaven; and at this sound the crowd gathered, all bewildered because each one heard his own language spoken.

—ACTS 2:5–6, NEB

Jerusalem was crowded. The city had pilgrims from all parts of the known world. They came seeking God. In the process they also brought to the city the most precious gift of all: their own heritages. Their heritage formed the framework with which these pilgrims understood reality and, at the same time, the window through which the world could reach their very souls. The heritage of a human being, when rightly understood, is a person's most precious means of communication and self-expression.

Thus, to address people in their native language is to engage in a sacred ritual. You are telling an individual that of all the diverse ethnic ways to express universal feelings, you are electing the way of that individual, of that culture, to communicate. Communication then becomes a ritual of reverence for that person's identity and world view. Conversation is possible because the mystery of life is shared in *known* and *familiar* ways.

So the pilgrims brought their souls and worlds to Jerusalem. Their common need brought them to that place. They sought God as the One who brought them forth into life, and nurtured them into adulthood. From their different ways of understanding the world they all longed for the presence of a God in whose presence reality made sense, and in whom life became meaningful. They never expected, however, that God would reach them at such an intimate level, in the most personal way possible.

Just as the Jerusalem pilgrims, we also come seeking meaning. We, too, carry around our identities and world views, unaware that they are our true gifts. We live in a world where automation demands uniformity, so we strive for predictable standards: food comes already prepared in our markets; clothes are ready-made in the stores; everything obeys certain patterns. The broader the uniformity, the shallower the understanding of life and its mysteries. (How many kids today could really appreciate the meaning it had for Joseph to receive a handmade, hand-painted coat of many colors?)

But then, the Spirit comes. And the Spirit of God is tremendously reverent! It speaks to each one of us according to our own heritage. It sings the songs we sing and dances the way we dance. In its presence, we are accepted as we are, as our innermost essence is. God elects our *own* way to communicate with us. And the most important lesson of Pentecost is that God does not choose one way at the cost of all others to communicate with human beings. God no longer bestows any culture with a spiritual superiority. Instead, in the Spirit of the season, all heritages receive God's revelation in words of grace, and are reconciled with God in *their uniqueness.*

In the days to come, God will continually pour out the Holy Spirit on all humankind, breaking the barriers of race, sex, class, age, and ethnocentric Christianity. No one can boast special election, and all partake of the same needed redemption.

Prayer

Spirit of the living God, bring us into the awareness of your reverence for humankind. Teach us to see beyond color and cultural barriers so that we can truly appreciate the gifts that are present in being unique. Come help us to speak to people in their own language, describing a world that can be home to them, and in the process take us home, too. Amen.

Hymn Suggestions

"O Spirit of the Living God"
"See How Great a Flame Aspires"
"Spirit of Life, in This New Dawn"

For Your Thoughts . . .

A Holy Spirit cannot be present in an egotistic encasement . . . you know yourself what stands in the way of the Pentecost Spirit. One does not want to change . . . and believe in the Lord Jesus Christ. It costs too much. It costs oneself.—*Emil Brunner*[13]

Action and Reflection

1. Pentecost celebrates the birth of the church and the unity of all people and cultures. Celebrate Pentecost by picking another country or culture to study during the next month. Pick a country or culture which is very different from yours. Put up a map that shows the home of the people you are studying. Check your library for books about the people you are studying. If you know someone from that culture, invite them to come talk to you about their home.

2. Talk about what makes your family/culture unique and special. Tell stories about your family's culture and origin.

3. Create symbols of your family and culture (special photographs, pictures symbolizing stories, and so on) and symbols of the country/culture you are studying (pictures, a globe, and so on). Place the symbols together in your worship space on a red flame made out of fabric.

4. Learn the following blessing in Portuguese or learn a simple blessing from the country you are studying. Use this blessing at your meals during the next week.

Bendição

Obrigado Deus por esta comida. Ao comermos celebramos irmãos e irmãs de outros paises e culturas. Obrigado pelos dons que nos fazem especiais como teus filhos e filhas. Amen.

(English Translation)
A Blessing

Thank you, God, for this food. As we eat this meal, we celebrate our brothers and sisters from other countries and cultures. Thank you for the gifts that make all of us unique children of yours. Amen.

A People with Skin on Them

Michael E. Williams
Tennessee

EZEKIEL 37:1–14
PENTECOST, YEAR B

God said to me, "Mortal man, the people of Israel are like these bones. They say that they are dried up, without any hope and with no future. So prophesy to my people Israel and tell them that I, the Lord God, am going to open their graves. I am going to take them out and bring them back to the land of Israel."
—EZEKIEL 37:11–12, TEV

A friend told me this story:

Awakening from a nightmare, a young girl called out in the night. Her mother heard her and came to offer comfort. After the terrors of the night had passed the mother and daughter talked.

Mother: I know how frightening dreams can be. But now you know you don't have to be afraid.

Daughter: But I was afraid. I was all alone.

Mother: You were alone in this room, but I was just down the hall. Besides, you know you are never really alone. God is always with you.

Daughter: I know, Mamma, but I needed somebody with skin on them.

Ezekiel tells this story:

God led me out into a valley covered with dry bones and asked the strangest question I ever heard: "Can these bones live?"

All I could say was, "Gracious, God, you know, 'cause I certainly don't."

And God told me to talk to the bones. "Tell them that I will breathe into them and put skin on them, and they'll live again," God said.

So, what was I to do? I talked to these dry bones and told them what God had said. And lo and behold, the bones began to shake and rattle and stand on their own. They came together. And suddenly from nowhere, it seems, they had skin on them.

Then God told me, "Call to the wind for breath."

So I called, and the wind came. Then the bones that were covered with skin began to breathe. It was an awesome sight.

That was when God said to me, "You know these aren't just dry bones, don't you? These are my people. Now you have a harder job. Call out to my people, who are as dead and dry as these bones. Tell them to

47

stand and breathe and come to life. Because, you see, I can't use old dead dry bones. I need a people with skin on them."

The poor, oppressed, and hungry people of our world know only too well the terrors of the day and night. But these are not imaginary fears. The prospects of hurt and even death are very much a part of everyday life. People who live under oppression need to know that God is with them in their suffering. They need to know that the prayers of concerned people are with them. But even more importantly, they need people with skin on them to respond to their needs.

God needs a people with skin on *us:* living, breathing people in service to the poor. Can *our* dry bones live?

Prayer
God of life, you comfort us like a mother comforts her daughter awakened from a nightmare. You call us to life as you called the dry bones together by Ezekiel's voice. Comfort those who hurt, who suffer and are afraid. Help us to be your people, a people with skin on them. Amen.

Hymn Suggestions
"Breathe on Me, Breath of God"
"God of Grace and God of Glory"
"Spirit of Faith, Come Down"

For Your Thoughts . . .
To the intellect, God is forever unknowable but to love, God is completely lovable and that by every separate individual. So much so that one living soul by itself, through its love, may know for itself God who is more than sufficient to fill all souls that exist.

—The Cloud of Unknowing[14]

Action and Reflection
1. Who in your community needs "somebody with skin on them"?

2. Pick one or more of these persons and decide how you can be right next to them. Together, make a plan for how can you be "somebody with skin on them" to the person who is hurting or oppressed. Here are some examples:

Help serve lunch in a soup kitchen.

Visit someone in jail who doesn't usually get visitors.

Assist a person who is ill or homebound in doing grocery shopping.

Visit a nursing home and request to see someone who has no family.

Volunteer to help in a shelter for the homeless.

3. Close with a time of prayer. If you are in a group, stand in a circle with arms wrapped around each other. Pray the prayer listed above.

Stop Fighting, and Know that I Am God

Beth A. Richardson
Tennessee

PSALM 46
SUNDAY BETWEEN JUNE 12 AND 18, YEAR B

The book of the Psalms is the hymnal of ancient Israel. These "hymns" were sung in the temple as a part of worship, much as we sing hymns in our worship services today. Particular psalms were used for occasions of praise, lament, thanksgiving, meditation, liturgy, and so on. Sometimes, they were accompanied by musical instruments or dance.

Today, we can use the Psalms as a part of our worship life. Psalm 46, speaking of God's ultimate strength over the events of the world, is a hymn for our troubled time. The Gentle Sculptor who fashioned this earth is also the Strong Protector who confronts humankind with its warring madness. "Stop fighting, and know that I am God."

Prayer

(normal speaking voice)

WOMEN: God is our refuge and strength,

MEN: a very present help in trouble.

WOMEN: Therefore we will not fear

(with gradual crescendo)
MEN: though the earth should change,

ALL: though the mountains shake in the heart of the sea;

WOMEN: though its waters roar and foam,

MEN: though the mountains tremble with its tumult.

(in a smooth whisper)
ALL: There is a river whose streams make glad the city of God, the holy habitation of the Most High.

(softly spoken)
MEN: God is in the midst of her, she shall not be moved;

WOMEN: God will help her right early.

(staccato)
MEN: The nations rage,   WOMEN: the kingdoms totter;

49

MEN: [God] utters his voice,   *WOMEN:*   the earth melts.

(smoothly)

ALL: The Lord of hosts is with us;
the God of Jacob is our refuge.

(with full voice, accenting every syllable and increasing in volume)

WOMEN: Come, behold the works of the Lord,
how [God] has wrought desolations in the earth.

MEN: [God] makes wars cease to the end of the earth;

WOMEN: [God] breaks the bow,   MEN: and shatters the spear,

ALL: [and] burns the chariots with fire!

(Pause)

(with quiet strength to the end)

WOMEN: "Be still, and know that I am God

MEN: I am exalted among the nations,

WOMEN: I am exalted in the earth!"

MEN: "Be still, and know that I am God."

ALL: The Lord of hosts is with us;
the God of Jacob is our refuge.
"Be still, and know that I am God."

—Psalm 46, RSV

Hymn Suggestions

"A Mighty Fortress Is Our God"
"God the Omnipotent"

For Your Thoughts . . .

Sometimes
I feel old
useless
and ugly
I reach and nothing comes
I speak and no one hears
I sing and no heart is moved
But then I pray
and Lord
You listen.
—Theresa Greenwood[15]

Action and Reflection

1. Read the psalm together as a litany of assurance of God's strength. Use the suggested divisions or make up your own (right and left, adults and children, and so on). Use the dynamics to make the psalm come alive. Read the lines as the dynamics suggest. Practice as an antiphonal choir several times before "singing" the psalm in your worship service.

2. Create an interpretive dance to accompany Psalm 46. As you read the psalm, identify the feelings that you have at different points in the poem. What are the movements that express those feelings? Put the movements together into a "dance" that can be done during the psalm reading.

God's Justice

John Carmody
Oklahoma

1 KINGS 21:1–21
SUNDAY BETWEEN JULY 3 AND 9, YEAR C

Ahab said to Elijah, "Have you found me, my enemy?" "I have found you," he said, "because you have sold yourself to do what is wrong in the eyes of the Lord. I will bring disaster upon you; I will sweep you away and destroy every mother's son of the house of Ahab in Israel, whether under protection of the family or not."
—1 KINGS 21:20–21, NEB

The story of Naboth the Jezreelite is a grim reminder that the Israelite prophets based their calls to social justice on very real evils in their society. Ahab and Jezebel, to be sure, are almost stock figures whom the writer uses to show the depravity that came when Israel turned aside from the God of Abraham and worshipped foreign gods. Nonetheless, most biblical scholars consider the murder of Naboth and the theft of his vineyard historical facts. The judgment of God that the prophet Elijah pronounces on Ahab and Jezebel essentially came to pass (Ahab was spared for a while but later died in battle), and so the worldly success that Israel enjoyed under Ahab's vigorous reign was condemned as wicked irreligion.

Naboth dies because he is faithful to Israel's tradition (Lev. 25) that patrimonial land should not be ceded away. Ahab is sullen (apparently habitually: see 1 Kings 20:43), like a child who cannot bear to have limits set to his will. His wife Jezebel, a Phoenician princess who energetically promoted the worship of Baal, her people's god, is willing to lie and murder to gain what Ahab wishes. The procedure that she arranges makes a mockery of Israelite legal custom, and we should mark well the complicity of the city elders who carry out Jezebel's evil command. The writer is not very subtly suggesting that corrupt rulers depend on cowardly followers to achieve their perverted ends. Elijah expresses the Israelite sense that injustice is trading one's self for base gain when he says to Ahab, "I have found you, because you have sold yourself to do what is evil in the sight of the Lord" (21:20 RSV; see also 21:25). The punishment said to come from God (being eaten by dogs) may strike us as barbaric, but, in the Israelite context of an eye for an eye, it is quite fitting.

For our contemporary purposes, the text perhaps best serves as a reminder that the arbitrary will of the powerful, who even today can commit gross evils in the pursuit of self-serving ends, is contained by God's justice. Every warmonger, industrial polluter, manufacturer who gouges the poor, and other gross violators of what should be will surely receive strict punishment. The cause of such evil-doing, this text suggests, is the false worship—the idolatry—that has taken people's hearts away from the true God. Were people today worshipping the mysterious love suggested by the wonders of creation and clarified by both the Israelite prophets and the cross of Christ, they would tremble to violate simple justice. Indeed, they would know a reality so much more precious than lands or riches that their greed and lust for power would seem ludicrous even to themselves.

Prayer

Dear God, let us not miss the desires of our own hearts that push us in the direction of Ahab and Jezebel. Let us see our own complicity in the sinful policies of our nation and the cowardice of our church. If we cannot be Elijah, empowered to condemn evil-doers to their face, let us at least support those who do prophesy. Be merciful to us all, O Lord; keep us under the cover of your justice; and let our hearts and hands go out to those victimized by evil, lest they despair of your reign.

Hymn Suggestions

"The Voice of God Is Calling"
"Where Cross the Crowded Ways of Life"

For Your Thoughts . . .

Hunger is the symptom. Lack of justice and human dignity is the real illness. At its root, the hunger/justice issue is a moral one.

There is no justice if rural people cannot make decisions for their own communities if they are exploited by corporations, land owners, or politicians.—*Thomas G. Pettepiece*[16]

Action and Reflection

1. The scripture talks about the idols which people put before God and the prophets who call us to put God first. Let us think of ways to honor the prophets of our day.

2. Pick a project or group which is prophesying and working for freedom today and think of ways to support them (Amnesty International, anti-apartheid movements, groups for the removal of food tax, hunger organizations, the sanctuary movement, and so on). Pick one activity to do as an individual, a family, or a group.

3. Celebrate our commitment to honor God's laws of justice by writing letters to your national or church leaders about issues which concern you.

Caring for Neighbors

Billie Nowabbi
Oklahoma

LUKE 10:25–37
SUNDAY BETWEEN JULY 10 AND 16, YEAR C

But a Samaritan, as he journeyed, came to where he was; and when he saw him, he had compassion, and went to him and bound up his wounds, pouring on oil and wine; then he set him on his own beast and brought him to an inn, and took care of him.

—LUKE 10:33–34, RSV

The scripture is a reminder that the teachings of Jesus command us to move beyond a mere feeling of compassion. We must venture into the act of removing the barriers that destroy and prevent the love of God in us, our neighbors, and our neighborhoods.

This parable illustrates the necessary quality of good will acted out by a Samaritan, one of a nation of people that was oppressed by the Jews. This Samaritan reached across the barrier to care for the oppressor. He came face to face with a real human situation. He accepted and acted upon the human need for care by binding up the wound, transporting the wounded stranger, and making provisions for his recovery.

In our modern situation, the parable could be told using a number of different actors in the two roles. Our world divisions lend many possibilities for this story.

Picture yourself as in great need of assistance, watching several respectable people pass by because of their fears of getting involved. Then you see a person who does not pass by, who does approach you, only to discover that the person is from a culture or country that your culture or country despises. This person not only stops, but pays his or her own money to help you on your way. Jesus says that this person is your neighbor more than all those who passed by.

Like the Samaritan, we are to live the answer by being the neighbor to the one who needs mercy. The good neighbor then, is one who shows mercy, who loves the neighbor. Our love for our neighbor is to reflect the love of God for us.

We are to cross our barriers to establish new relations of caring and to begin God's work of reconciliation in a world of brokenness and isolation. There can be no holding back because we are different, have limited resources or are not of the same religion.

We cannot choose those whom we will serve because Christ has already selected our brothers and sisters through our moment by moment encounters with persons having needs and concerns.

We must do more than talk. Jesus told us, "Go and do likewise." We must act out and reflect the love of God. If God's love is in us, we cannot pass by in the face of human need as did the priest and Levite. The God who cares for us is also worthy of our services and love. Our love for God is the motive that prevents us from passing by.

Prayer

Lord, give us the mind to be more open to your sons and daughters, a heart that is willing to respond to your love and grace. Help us not to pass by but to let others see you at work in this world. In Jesus Christ we pray. Amen.

Hymn Suggestions

"Where Cross the Crowded Ways of Life"
"In Christ There Is No East or West"
"O Brother Man, Fold to Thy Heart"

For Your Thoughts . . .

We use God's love to prove our love for God in action through our service to the poor—the lepers, the dying, the crippled, the unloved, or the uncared for whoever they may be. For us they are Christ in the distressing disguise of the poorest of the poor.—*Mother Teresa*[17]

Action and Reflection

1. Jesus tells the story of the Good Samaritan to answer the question, "Who is my neighbor?" How would you answer that question today? Retell the story of the Good Samaritan as it might take place today.

2. Get a pen pal from the Soviet Union or another country at odds with yours by writing that country's embassy in your country. Think about how you are a neighbor to someone who lives so far away.

3. Jesus tells the hearers of the story to "go and do likewise." What are the ways that you can "do likewise"? Make a list of three things that you will do this week to be a good neighbor.

Visions of Light

Hoyt L. Hickman
Tennessee

MATTHEW 17:1–9
MARK 9:2–9
LUKE 9:28–36
AUGUST 6, YEAR A, B, OR C

And after six days Jesus took with him Peter and James and John, and led them up a high mountain apart by themselves; and he was transfigured before them, and his garments became glistening, intensely white, as no fuller on earth could bleach them. . . . And a cloud overshadowed them, and a voice came out of the cloud, "This is my beloved Son; listen to him."

—MARK 9:2–3, 7, RSV

Note: While the Common Calendar designates the Last Sunday after Epiphany as Transfiguration, August 6 is the historic date for celebrating the Transfiguration and is still on the calendars of the Roman Catholic and Episcopal Churches. Since August 6, or the previous Sunday, is a time when we appropriately remember Hiroshima, it is a powerful juxtoposition of images to view this in the light of the Transfiguration.

Two momentous events are commemorated each year on August 6. Each is a vision of dazzling light, followed by an overshadowing cloud. Each is said to be a vision of the future of the human race. If we take either vision to heart, our lives will never be the same again.

One is the destruction of Hiroshima on August 6, 1945, by an atomic bomb—a dazzling fireball like a thousand suns, followed by an over-shadowing mushroom cloud. Beyond the horror of the event itself is the knowledge that the human race now has the power to destroy itself. Bertrand Russell said in despair that humanity "has never refrained from any folly of which it was capable." If this is true and cannot be changed, then in looking at Hiroshima we have seen the future of the human race—extinction.

This vision can make us fatalistic, living for the moment or making only short-range plans, hoping for as much as possible out of life before the end comes. We become like the driver of an auto on a collision course who panics, freezes at the wheel, and turns the fear of accident into self-fulfilling prophecy.

But August 6 commemorates another event, the Transfiguration, that gives us an opposite vision of the future. Like Peter, James, and John, we can see Christ upon the mountain top—his face shining like the sun, his garments dazzling white as light. With Christ are Moses, giver of the moral law, whose face shone when he was with God face to face, and Elijah, the prophet whom God took up into heaven on a fiery chariot. After the display of light, we are overshadowed by a bright cloud that is the glory of God, saying: "This is my beloved Son; listen to him."

This vision is God's conformation of who Jesus is, given at a time when the disciples were unable to face the coming suffering and crucifixion. It is a foretaste of Christ's resurrection and exaltation. It is God's assurance that Jesus is not a deluded idealist who will be destroyed by the cruel world but, rather, that Jesus and what he (and Moses and the prophets) taught will be vindicated in God's ultimate victory.

If we are guided and empowered by this vision, we can persevere in our work for peace and justice, no matter what happens. If we meet with successes, even if they be small and temporary, they can be signs to us of glory to come, as was the disciples' mountaintop experience of Jesus' Transfiguration. We can be prepared for terrible defeats, like the shattering experiences of the disciples as the mount of Transfiguration was followed by the mount of Calvary, because we are confident that beyond lies God's victory.

In that confidence we are able to "be steadfast, immovable, always abounding in the work of the Lord, knowing that in the Lord our labor is not in vain" (1 Cor. 15:58, RSV).

Prayer

O God, you are with us both in times of joy and in times of tragedy. We come before you on this day that symbolizes both the best and the worst in humanity. We remember with sorrow the victims of the bombings of Hiroshima and Nagasaki. For the survivers who live in terror around the world, we ask your comfort and your courage. Teach us to live in peace, trusting in the vision of Christ on the mountaintop, dazzling in your light. Guide our journey toward the glory of that mountain, toward your victory, toward a peaceful humankind. Amen.

Hymn Suggestions

"God the Omnipotent"
"This Is My Song"
"All Hail the Power of Jesus' Name"

For Your Thoughts . . .

God is waiting still to find a believing community who will hear the word and get the message. . . . We all . . . are called to see in the massive mysteries of creation the design of a God who is just, and loving, and moving towards his people in power.—*Erik Routley*[18]

Action and Reflection

1. In Japan, a national symbol of peace and hope is the origami crane. This symbol appears in the story of the life of a little girl named Sadako Sasaki. Read the story, *Sadako and the Thousand Paper Cranes* by Eleanor Coerr. Learn to fold paper cranes and fold some to put in your worship center. (Check with your library for books that will show you how to fold cranes.)

2. Plan a worship time for August 6.

—Have a Feast of Remembrance for those who died in the bombing. Plan a simple meal of rice, soup, egg rolls, and bean cakes.

—Decorate your table with paper cranes and a special candle to burn during the meal.

—For your blessing, learn "Song for Sadako," included below. (The words to this song are based on the statue of Sadako in Hiroshima Peace Park.)

—Talk about your feelings concerning the events that we observe on August 6. What are your hopes and fears about the meaning of Hiroshima and Nagasaki? What does the Transfiguration add to your hopes and fears for the world?

—Close your worship time by singing "Song for Sadako" and praying the prayer above.

Written as a class project "Share The Sunlight" Seminar, Religious Studies Department, Villanova University, Villanova, Pennsylvania.

Mary Lu Walker and Friends
July 1985

58

Wilderness Journey

Walter Brueggemann
From *Living Toward a Vision*

EXODUS 16:2–18, 31
SUNDAY BETWEEN AUGUST 14 AND 20, YEAR A

When the dew evaporated, there was something thin and flaky on the surface of the desert. It was as delicate as frost. When the Israelites saw it, they didn't know what it was and asked each other, "What is it?"
Moses said to them, "This is the food that the Lord has given you to eat."
—EXODUS 16:14–15, TEV

When the Israelites left Egypt, they thought they were on the way to the promised land, for that is what God said (Ex. 3:8). . . . And they were on the way to promise. But the promise characteristically leads through the wilderness, and sometimes the stay is long. It is important that wilderness always be linked to the promised land. The reality of wilderness is always in the context of the vision. . . . The dynamic of wilderness and promise is not unlike the "in the world, but not of it" of the Fourth Gospel. Israel is *in* the wilderness but *of* the promised land.

For the rest, you know about the wilderness.

1. It is a place where there is no visible supply of bread, water, or meat. *Shalom* personhood means to go readily and joyously to where the visible supplies do not exist. Wilderness is the absence of all conventional support systems. And when they are absent, it is important not to be *of* the wilderness, even if *in* it. . . . We can scarcely do the kind of living or ministering to which we are called if the pressures of the present consume us. But they will not when we know ourselves *of* the promised land.

2. The wilderness is without visible support, but it is also the place where ample supplies of manna are given every day. It is a place that seems to be without support and that surely lacks the support to which we are accustomed. But being there leads to a new and unexpected awareness that within the wilderness there are supports. Bread is given. Water does break forth. Quail do fall and there is meat. And the wilderness theme runs ahead to Jesus' teaching: "Do not be anxious, your Father knows your need." The trick is to get our minds and hearts off our insecurity and anxiety long enough to trust God.

59

3. Which permits us to say that the wilderness is the place where *shalom* persons come face to face with the daily faithfulness of the Lord, who shapes things for well-being. This is not to say that the wilderness is all sweetness and light. The biblical memory is filled with complaint and grievance and dissatisfaction. . . . The surprise of the wilderness is that just when Israel thought itself forgotten and abandoned, just then God appears, faithful in life-giving ways. So the great gift of wilderness is not just that there are no visible supports or that there are surprising gifts. It is that in the wilderness, unencumbered, Israel meets the One who gives a name and an identity. All the "stuff" is cut through; and there is meeting. *Shalom* persons know that it is meeting and not stuff, "Thou" and not "It," that gives energy and power to our personhood.[19]

Prayer

Leader: God of Moses, we are people of the wilderness.

People: Help us to go joyously to the places where there are no visible means of support.

Leader: God of Miriam, we are people of faith.

People: We trust in your manna to feed and nourish us.

Leader: God of the promised land, we are shalom people.

People: We follow you to the wilderness, using only what we need, and participating as partners in your vision of justice.

All: Amen.

Hymn Suggestion

"Guide Me, O Thou Great Jehovah"

For Your Thoughts . . .

Lord, the hunger problem seems hopeless to many, the victims and the by-standers but hope needs opportunity and you have given me now an unparallelled chance to be a part of conquering this condition conscious of your presence which supplies me with strength and with hope.

—*Arthur Simon*[20]

Action and Reflection

1. The story from Exodus 16 tells us that in times of difficulty, God provides all that we need. It also tells us that we should use only as much as we need and no more. What are the ways that God has provided manna for you? Are there times that you use more than you need? Talk about how you can, like Moses instructed, "gather only as much as you need."

2. Are there ways that God is calling you to put yourself in the wilderness (places without guaranteed support)? As you strive to grow in

shalom, discern whether there are ways that you are being called to the wilderness. Are you being called to:

Deeper involvement in particular issues by participating in demonstrations or other activities?

Become involved in civil disobedience for peace, human rights in South Africa, or other issues?

Urge your local congregation to become a part of the Sanctuary movement?

Visit a country in need of justice and peace to learn about how you can influence the government and the church to be peacemakers?

Cost of Discipleship

Clarence Jordan and Bill Lane Doulos
From *Cotton Patch Parables of Liberation*

LUKE 14:25–33
SUNDAY BETWEEN SEPTEMBER 4 AND 10, YEAR C

Now great multitudes accompanied [Jesus]; and he turned and said to them, "If anyone comes to me and does not hate his own father and mother and wife [and husband] and children and brothers and sisters, yes, and even his own life, he cannot be my disciple."

—LUKE 14:25–26, RSV

Quite a crowd was trailing Jesus, and he turned and said to them, "If anyone is considering joining me, and does not break their attachment for father and mother and wife and children and brothers and sisters, indeed—for their own life—they simply cannot belong to my fellowship. Anyone who does not accept their own lynching and fall in behind me cannot belong to my fellowship.

"If any of you were intending to put up a building, wouldn't you first sit down and figure out the cost, so you could see if you had enough to finish it? Otherwise, you might lay out the foundation, and because you didn't have funds to go any further, people would begin making cracks about you, saying, 'This one is a great hand at starting things, but can't carry through on them.'

"Or suppose a king were going out to battle against another king, wouldn't he first sit down and determine whether or not, with his ten thousand men, he could face an enemy of twenty thousand? If he figures he can't, then while there is still distance between them, he should send a delegation to seek for terms of peace.

"So that's the way it is with you. Everyone of you who doesn't throw in their entire fortune cannot belong to my fellowship." Luke 14:25–33.

These parables of the incomplete building and the king's warfare point to the necessity for understanding the ultimate cost of discipleship. Jesus wants us to be fully aware of the implications of being children of God's grace. The context of these two parables outlines two of the requirements: "Anyone who does not accept their own lynching" and "who doesn't throw in their entire fortune cannot belong to my fellowship." Are we that serious about entering the Reign of God that we sever ourselves from family ties, earthly security, and all of the dreams that we

62

nurture for ourselves? Are we prepared to throw everything up in the air, including our schooling and our careers, our possessions and our ideas? Or are there certain relationships and realities that control us? God is giving us fair warning that God will touch us at every point to test whether our commitment is total. We can't bluff our way into God's family. And we will be laughingstock to both God and ourselves if we permit anything to separate us from the consuming priority of God's Reign. Like the plight of the empty house, our fate then will be worse than if we had never taken Jesus seriously in the first place.[21]

Prayer

Jesus has said that for anyone to follow him, that person must give up their ties. Those words are difficult for us to hear, dear God, for we are very attached to our relationships, our possessions, our lives. Give us wisdom to understand the costs that you demand of us when we choose to become a disciple of Jesus. Give us courage to face the consequences of being your presence in the world. And give us comfort when the way is long and hard. We pray in your name. Amen.

Hymn Suggestions

"Are Ye Able?"
"Take My Life, and Let It Be Consecrated"
"Jesus Calls Us O'er the Tumult"

For Your Thoughts . . .

If we truly believe that Jesus Christ has broken the authority and dominion of the Corporate and personal powers of death in the world . . . the community of believers must expect to find themselves at variance with the social consensus, the political conformity.—*Jim Wallis*[22]

Action and Reflection

1. In the story from Luke, Jesus is talking about the costs to anyone who chooses to follow him. What does it mean to break attachments to our earthly ties . . . our family, possessions, our schooling . . . in order to follow Jesus?

2. Do you know anyone who has given up something to follow Jesus' teaching? Ask them to talk with you about what they lost . . . and what they gained.

3. Can you think of the consequences that you as an individual or a family might experience (or have experienced) as a result of your work for a just world?

4. Close this time with the prayer listed above. If you are in a group, say the prayer in a hug circle.

A Warning About Being Partial

James Earl Massey
Alabama

JAMES 2:1–17
SUNDAY BETWEEN SEPTEMBER 11 AND 17, YEAR B

> *If a man with gold rings and in fine clothing comes into your assembly, and a poor man in shabby clothing also comes in, and you pay attention to the one who wears fine clothing and say, "Have a seat here, please," while you say to the poor man, "Stand there," or "Sit at my feet," have you not made distinctions among yourselves, and become judges with evil thoughts?*
>
> —JAMES 2:2–4, RSV

The writer of the passage was a teacher concerned with helping believers adhere fully to Christian faith and practice. In promoting a thoroughgoing commitment, the writer supplies admonitions and pastoral encouragement for living by "the rules."

The passage before us addresses attitudes toward wealth. Having already advised the poor against seeking wealth as an ultimate good, and the rich against hoarding wealth as an everlasting boon, the writer now offers advice against being partial and seeking or giving privileged treatment as a result of social standing as displayed by possessions.

This word about divisive distinctions between social classes reminds us of our ties to one another through a basic humanity under God. We are reminded that class lines should not affect the way we relate to each other—whether during the times of gathering for worship or after such times. The Christian faith levels all believers; it allows no authoritative pride of place by the rich over the poor. The passage rebukes such selfishness and unwarranted distinctions.

The rich-poor problem is treated several places in James. Some of these passages give a radical criticism of wealth and affluence, but largely because arrogance seems to follow pride in possessing, and social privilege is often expected when one enjoys economic advantage. The fact is wealth can lead one astray, seducing one by a false sense of self-importance, unless one lives by a higher attitude of regard and recognized relationship. The crucial messages in our passage are that Christian faith demands a heart and that love gives proof of itself in unselfish and impartial deeds. A common faith and an open fellowship go together. True love will eagerly seek to reduce the problems and ills that people suffer; it will never increase them.

Our passage addresses the great issue of how we will regard each other—and our motives for doing so. It is a clear call to live by a higher attitude than partiality represents. It is a word against arrogance, pride, and unwarranted class lines.

> The Lord said,
> "Say, 'We' ";
> But I shook my head,
> Hid my hands tight behind my back, and said,
> Stubbornly,
> "I."
>
> The Lord said,
> "Say, 'We' ";
> But I looked upon them, grimy and all awry.
> Myself in all those twisted shapes? Ah, no!
> Distastefully I turned my head away,
> Persisting,
> "They."
>
> The Lord said,
> "Say, 'We' ";
> And I,
> At last,
> Richer by a hoard
> Of years
> And tears,
> Looked in their eyes and found the heavy word
> That bent my neck and bowed by head:
> Like a shamed schoolboy then I mumbled low,
> "We,
> Lord."[23]

Prayer

O God, help me to read the truth about myself and others with open, regarding eyes. Keep me back from the sin of being partial. Let me not judge, except between good and evil. Let me not fail to love and relate in keeping with the spirit of Jesus, my Lord. In his name I pray. Amen.

Hymn Suggestions

"The Voice of God Is Calling"
"Where Cross the Crowded Ways of Life"
"God of Grace and God of Glory"

For Your Thoughts . . .

"The presence of God with us" still happens when Christians participate with others in bringing relief to the hungry and justice to the oppressed.

—Shirley J. Hickman[24]

Action and Reflection

1. How does society favor the rich and disfavor the poor? Look in a newspaper and cut out examples of how the poor are disfavored and the rich favored.

2. Take a walk or a drive in a different part of the city or area than where you live. What things are different or the same? (Be sure to notice things like roads, sidewalks, or stores.) Are any of the differences signs of society's partiality for the rich?

3. Try to think what it would be like to have less money than you have. List the ten favorite things you, your family, or your group do for fun. Which things could you not do if you did not have money?

Sojourn to Shalom

Roy I. Sano
Colorado

MICAH 1:2, 2:1–10
SUNDAY BETWEEN OCTOBER 9 AND 15, YEAR C

How terrible it will be for those who lie awake and plan evil! When morning comes, as soon as they have the chance, they do the evil they planned. When they want fields, they seize them; when they want houses, they take them. No man's family or property is safe.

—MICAH 2:1–2, TEV

The prophet Micah saw peace coming when wrongs are righted. Because sin and evil abounded in his day, he recognized that God had much to do before shalom would prevail.

While he acknowledged evil permeating all his people, Micah directed his severest criticism against the rich leaders in the cities who exploited the poor in small towns. Merchants extracted more than their share by falsifying weights and measures. Defrauded villagers fell into debt and heartless creditors foreclosed their farms. Those removed from their lands were denied shelter; women and children were left without protection. Micah not only saw in these practices predators who preyed on their victims like ravenous beasts, he condemned these acts as violations of the glory of God.

Despite the exploitation, indulgent priests and prophets intoxicated people with their pronouncements of "peace" and "security." Micah by contrast said, "Arise and go, for this is no place to rest; because of uncleanness that destroys with a grievous destruction" (2:10). The faithful prophet saw the Holy One offended by unholy acts.

Micah proclaimed that, as the righteous and rectifying One, God will go on the offense against the recalcitrant exploiters at home and the destructive invaders from abroad. He prophesied that the Redeemer who delivered the Hebrews from their enslavement in Egypt will liberate them again from their oppressors and intimidators. The God Mighty-to-Save "will tread . . . iniquities under foot (and) cast all . . . sins into the depth of the sea" (7:19), much as Yahweh had done to Pharaoh's legion who threatened to overtake the children of Israel on their flight from bondage and take them back into slavery. God will feed and care for the flock like a shepherd, just as the Gracious Provider sustained the people in their pilgrimage to the Promised Land. The Great Shepherd of the sheep will come from the outlying town of Bethlehem which was "little . . . among the clans of Judah" (5:2).

Micah promised that the people will "dwell secure" and rest unafraid in their vineyards and groves when their former enemies heed God's word and convert their weapons into constructive tools. God will also remove the Hebrews' own instruments of warfare. Thus, after evil is redressed and sin rectified, God will establish peace where righteousness and justice prevail.

It is not enough today simply to prevent a situation from escalating into a shooting war, though we cannot overlook this task. If unrighteousness permeates societies and injustices dominate interactions among the people, the awesome and compassionate Rectifier will act. Until healing, health, and life prevail, the living and holy God will not rest. The Bible invites us to join Micah in witnessing to this God; Micah invites us to join this unrelenting God in this ongoing work. Arise, let us sojourn with this God to shalom.

Prayer   (Divide people into two sides, each reading its respective part.)

Left: Righteous and gracious God, pour out your Holy Spirit, who stirs us to long and labor for freedom;

Right: freedom from the exploitation and intimidation which dominate your creatures on this fragile island in the universe.

Left: We join you even now in your unrelenting work of rectifying wrong inside us and among us

Right: so that all your creatures may dwell secure with one another.

All: May we thus fulfill your vision of a new heaven and a new earth. In Christ's name we pray. Amen.

Hymn Suggestions

"O Young and Fearless Prophet"
"God Hath Spoken by His Prophets"

For Your Thoughts . . .

We are still beset by the tendency of those who are presently privileged to ignore or treat in a surface way the problems faced by those who are not privileged.—*Peggy Billings*[25]

Action and Reflection

1. What are the signs of God's work for shalom today? Make a list of shalom signs. What are the signs of injustice in our world today? Make a list of signs of injustice.

2. Liturgy of shalom:
Do the following worship liturgy together. Ask different persons to read the three parts for leaders.

—Sing one of the hymns listed above.

—First Leader: Gracious Father, we thank you for the signs of shalom that we see in your world. We see . . . (everyone help list the signs of shalom.)

—Second Leader: We are sorry, Loving Mother, that there are many places in the world where injustice dominates shalom. We see . . . (everyone help list signs of injustice.)

—Third Leader: Lover of Justice, we offer ourselves as your hands and your feet. We promise to work for shalom in your world. (Everyone list one way they will work for shalom.)

—Close with the prayer listed above or the Lord's Prayer

When Belief Becomes Reality

Irene Boyd
Tennessee

MARK 10:35–45
SUNDAY BETWEEN OCTOBER 16 AND 22, YEAR B

Whoever would be great among you must be your servant, and whoever would be first among you must be slave of all. For the Son of man also came not to be served but to serve, and to give his life as a ransom for many.

—MARK 10:43B–45, RSV

"Are you able to drink the cup that I drink." The words kept running on in her mind like a scratched record as she tried not to think of the consequences of saying yes.

Elizabeth definitely was not the martyr type. Now here she was sitting before Mr. Meyer, the company president, who had just offered her the opportunity of her career. "With the increase in minimum wage and state taxes, we can no longer operate here and make the large profits we've had in the past. I'd like you to explore some of the third world countries for a place for us to relocate—a place where we can find some cheap labor and the government will be glad to accommodate us. You do well on this project and you'll go far in the company."

"But what about the workers here. What will happen to them?" She couldn't believe she was asking this question when she should be jumping at the opportunity Mr. Meyer was offering her.

"They have my sympathy," he replied matter-of-factly, "but, as you know, we've got to maximize our profits. Look at it this way—we'll give people in the third world a chance to work and to better their lives."

"But we'll still be exploiting them," she blurted.

"Do you want the job?" he interrupted curtly. "Or would you like to be among the workers you're so concerned about?"

O God! she thought. I shouldn't have to be making choices like this.

"Are you able to drink the cup?" Why were those words haunting her?

All her life she had been ambitious, had overcome many obstacles along the way, had been moving toward such an opportunity. And she was proud of the fact that she had not compromised her ideals and principle. God was an important dimension of her life. Years ago she had said yes to following Jesus, yes to his vision of the reign of God. It's so easy to say yes to a vision, she reflected, but when reality presents itself, it's another matter. I hadn't expected it to come to this.

People won't understand if I say no to this chance. They'll think I'm a fool, and they'll be right. It's absurd to think Jesus would expect me to sacrifice my career over this, she argued with herself.

"Anyone among you who aspires to greatness must serve the rest. Are you able to drink the cup?"

They're harsh words, she thought. I can't take them.

"They're life-giving. Trust me." The words swelled from the depths of her soul. She said her yes again—but this time not so naively.

"I will not take the job, Mr. Meyer. It is wrong, and I won't participate in such injustice." She got up to leave.

"You are a fool, Elizabeth," he uttered uncomprehendingly. "You've just thrown away your life."

"No, Mr. Meyer. I've just drunk it. Good-bye."

Prayer

O God, who showed us through Jesus what it means to be servant, grant us wisdom to see those places we are to follow you. Challenge us, as members of families, churches, and communities, to be servants of peace and keepers of righteousness. And when we must make choices which take us on unknown paths, hold us in your arms of comfort and courage. In Christ's name we pray. Amen.

Hymn Suggestions

"Are Ye Able?"
"We Give Thee But Thine Own"

For Your Thoughts . . .

The Christian ethic claims that it is more important to love than to survive, than to assure our survival by careful, selective, exclusion of those parts of the human species who seem to us obviously maladaptive and a burden to us in our attempts to survive.—*Dieter T. Hessel*[26]

Action and Reflection

1. The word *service* comes from a Latin word meaning "slave." When Jesus talks of being a servant, he is talking about going beyond what has to be done, of giving extra of one's time and energy and resources, of making a sacrifice. How are you in service to your family? To your community?

2. On a big sheet of paper, draw a family crest of service. Divide the crest into two parts, for family and for community. Each person list or draw pictures of how they will be in service to the family and to the community. (Some things you may already be doing and other things may be new.) Hang the crest in a place in your home.

3. Following the same processes as above, draw a crest of service for your church. Divide the crest into parts representing the congregation and the community.

Love that Transforms

Will Campbell

From *Race and the Renewal of the Church*

LUKE 19:1–10

SUNDAY BETWEEN OCTOBER 30 AND NOVEMBER 5, YEAR C

Zacchaeus stood up and said to the Lord, "Listen, sir! I will give half my belongings to the poor, and if I have cheated anyone, I will pay him back four times as much."
Jesus said to him, "Salvation has come to this house today, for this man, also, is a descendant of Abraham. The Son of Man came to seek and to save the lost."
—LUKE 19:8–10, TEV

Jesus both loved and called to accountability the most despised of his day . . . the tax collectors. Will Campbell, a civil rights activist, writes in the early 1960s about one of the most despised in that day, the racist.

The church must be concerned with the segregationist not only because he/she is within the institution, but especially and above all because he/she too is a child of God. The church cannot force the racist out of its fellowship by any arbitrary or highhanded discipline. The church must understand the segregationist, but at the same time it must not permit understanding . . . to mean that its own policy becomes silence or inaction. . . . Jesus understood the real condition of the people of Jerusalem, but the knowledge that certain social and political factors played a role in the popular customs and ethos of the city did not keep him from entering Jerusalem and turning it upside down.

. . . Those of us who consider ourselves the children of light with respect to our attitudes and practices in race relations must ask ourselves what happened in our lives to make us so different from the racist. Even if God laid God's hands on us, even if some are chosen, to what credit can we claim, what reason have we to boast, and what right to condemn? Somehow we cannot hate the racist, for most of us do not know how or when we left the racist's ranks, if we have left them at all.

I have seen and known the resentment of the racist, the hostility, the frustration, the need for someone upon whom to lay blame and to punish. I know he/she is mistaken, misguided and willfully disobedient, but somehow I am not able to distinguish between the racist and myself. My sins may not be the same, but they are no less real and no less heinous. Perhaps I have been too close to this person. Perhaps if I had not heard the anguished cry when the rains didn't come in time to save the cotton, if I had not felt the severity of the economic deprivation, if I had not looked upon their agony on Christmas Eve while I, their six-year-old child, feigning sleep, waited for a Santa who would never come; if I had not been one with them through these gales of tragedy, I would be able to condemn him/her without hesitation. . . . Perhaps I would not pity the racist as much if I were not from the same place.

But the church must not pity the racist. It must love and redeem him/her. It must somehow set the racist free. With the same love that it is commanded to shower upon the innocent victim of the frustration and hostility, the church must love the racist. Moreover, the church is called to love those who use and exploit both the racists and their victims for personal wealth and political gain. The church must stand in love and judgment upon the victim, the victimized, and those, both black and white, who exploit both, for they are all the children of God.[27]

Prayer

God of compassion, we confess that we often function out of judgment rather than love. We see ourselves as better than others, overlooking our own sins and shortcomings. Make us a forgiving people, concerned with the gifts and possibilities of our sisters and brothers in the world. Teach us to live together in love, gently helping each other along the way toward lives of peace and justice. We ask these things in your name. Amen.

Hymn Suggestions

"Depth of Mercy"
"Jesus, the Sinner's Friend, to Thee"

For Your Thoughts . . .

Genuine forgiveness is participation, reunion, overcoming the powers of estrangement. And only because this is so, does forgiveness make love possible.—*Paul Tillich*[28]

Action and Reflection

1. Who are the people who are hard to love because of their actions in the world? (The people who enforce unjust policies, those whose political or theological beliefs are different from yours, the classmate whose job is to keep an eye on the class while the teacher is out of the room?)

2. In the story of Zacchaeus, Jesus gave us an example of how to treat the ones we despise. What are the ways that we can love the people we have listed above, while still hoping for their transformation to a world of justice and shalom?

Help each other think of ways to love others while holding them to accountability.

Choose one action that will help you manifest this love and practice it for the next two weeks. For example, spend some time with such people to get to know them better. Or, if the person or group lives far away, do not make any bad comments about that person or persons for two weeks. Instead, try to think about that person's feelings or thoughts as a human being. (At the end of two weeks, talk about what you learned, ways you feel different or the same. Is this an action you would like to continue?)

Giving and Receiving

Naomi P. F. Southard
California

MARK 12:41–44
SUNDAY BETWEEN NOVEMBER 6 AND 12, YEAR B

[Jesus] called his disciples to him. "I tell you this," he said: "this poor widow has given more than any of the others; for those others who have given had more than enough, but she, with less than enough, has given all that she had to live on."
—MARK 12:43–44, NEB

Recently, I had the opportunity to lead a workshop on missions for high school students. The young people had a positive view of missions. Among their chief concerns were famine in central Africa, natural disasters around the world, and the need for medical aid in war-torn countries. The students were aware of the privileges and comforts they enjoy, and were eager to help those who have fewer resources, to express the love of the gospel by sharing some of their abundance.

During this time, I asked the teenagers, "How can the poor be in mission to us—what can we receive or learn from them?" This question had never occurred to the students. Like many of us, they were all too accustomed to seeing themselves as the ones who have "something to give" and others as being "needy"; the young people could not easily comprehend the ways in which they needed the gifts of the poor. The attitude such thinking conveys puts others in the utterly dependent position of receiving, cutting off the possibility of the givers learning from those whose faith has been tested and strengthened in difficult circumstances.

Today's brief passage in Mark challenges us to look deeply into the values we have about giving—and receiving. First, we must ask about the quality of our own giving. Do you see yourself as being like the rich who "cast in much" to the treasury or like the widow who "cast in all she had"—or neither? This passage emphasizes the blessedness of giving as much as is possible according to your resources.

Second, we must learn to value the giver and the gift. Whether large or small, it is the sacrificial generosity of the giver which measures the value of the gift. Gifts are not only money or other material resources. Do we honor the contributions of wisdom, humility, vision, thankfulness, wholehearted participation and limitation when they are given by the elderly, those with handicapping conditions, or the socially or politically ostracized? The gospel calls us to cultivate a community of faith that recognizes the potential of each person to give and has the insight to appreciate diverse gifts and givers.

If we are to be truly in mission, we must strive to live out our Christian faith through sacrificial giving and with the knowledge that we cannot begin to transform this world's violence and despair without recognizing and using the gifts of every person in the community. Two phrases which express this idea are "mutuality in mission" and "ecumenical sharing of resources." As we learn our role in giving and receiving, as we share the good news with persons who suffer from spiritual, material, or social degradation, we can celebrate an equal partnership in this mission with all who have experienced God's love.

Prayer

Leader: We are thankful, God, for the blessings that you have given us.
People: For friends, for food, for shelter, we give you thanks.
Leader: We are thankful, Creator, for the gifts that we are able to give to others.
People: For material resources, for knowledge, for compassion, we give you thanks.
Leader: We are thankful, loving Parent, for the blessings all as human beings may receive from and give to each other.
People: For wisdom, for smiles, for humility, for vision, we give you thanks.
Leader: Fashion us after the widow who "cast in all she had."
People: Make us, with all your children, equal partners in mission.
All: Amen.

Hymn Suggestions

"Take My Life, and Let It Be Consecrated"
"We Give Thee but Thine Own"

For Your Thoughts . . .

Affluent social classes are engaged in the ultimate idolatory: they seek access to God in rituals that reinforce injustice. Their exploitation of the poor makes their religiosity a mockery.—*Jack A. Nelson*[29]

Action and Reflection

1. The Protestant church's early mission work was funded primarily by women's organizations called Cent Societies or Mite Societies. This fact is especially dramatic when we realize that all many women were able to give were small coins, pennies. (Most women were not permitted to have much money of their own. Fathers or husbands controlled income and expenditures.) But pennies add up to dollars! Observe this principle by making a "Mite Box" out of a jar or can. Put it on your table and add to it daily. Decide together where the money should go.

2. Are you better at giving or receiving? What do you give to others in your society? What do you receive from them? What gifts do you receive from the poor and the dispossessed in your society? Make a list of the things that you receive from those who are considered to be around the edges of your society. Keep the list in your worship center to remind you to be thankful for these gifts, which are often forgotten or ignored.

Notes

■

1. Thelma Stevens, *Legacy for the Future* (New York: Women's Divison, Board of Global Ministries, The United Methodist Church, 1978), p. 53.

2. Marianne Katoppo, *Compassionate and Free* (Maryknoll, NY: Orbis Books, 1980), p. 17.

3. Peter Matheson, *A Just Peace* (New York: Friendship Press, 1981), p. 6.

4. Joseph B. Fabry, *The Pursuit of Meaning* (Boston: Beacon Press, 1968), p. 141.

5. Howard Thurman, *With Head and Heart* (New York: Harcourt Brace Jovanovich, Inc., 1979), p. 114.

6. Daniel H. Evans, "Prayer for a Rescue Not Always Wanted", *alive now!* March/April 1983, p. 8.

7. *The Twelve Prophets* (London: The Sonica Press, 1948), p. 154.

8. Martin Luther King, Jr., *Martin Luther King, Jr.: Pastor . . . Revolutionary . . .*, SCLC mlks E 6905, sound disk.

9. Paul Tournier, *Reflections* (New York: Harper & Row, 1976), p. 171.

10. Martin Buber, *Ten Rungs: Hasidic Sayings* (New York: Schocken Books, 1973), p. 101.

11. Aly Wassil, *The Wisdom of Christ* (New York: Harper & Row, 1965), p. 35.

12. William Sloan Coffin, Jr., "Introduction," in *Peace in Search of Makers*, Jane Rockman, ed. (New York: Judson Press, 1979), pp. 10–11.

13. Emil Brunner, *I Believe In the Living God*, translated by John Holder (Philadelphia: Westminster Press, 1961), pp. 133–4.

14. *The Cloud of Unknowing*, Clifton Walters, trans. (Middlesex, England: Penguin Books, 1979), p. 63.

15. Theresa Greenwood, *Psalms of A Black Mother* (Anderson, Indiana: Warner Press, 1970), p. 32.

16. Thomas Pettepiece, *Visions of a World Hungry* (Nashville: The Upper Room, 1979), p. 79.

17. Mother Teresa, *My Life For the Poor*, ed. by Jose Luis Gonzales-Balada and Janet N. Playfoot (New York: Harper & Row, 1985), p. 18.

18. Erik Routley, *Saul among the Prophets* (Nashville: The Upper Room, 1972), pp. 7–8.

19. Walter Brueggemann, *Living Toward a Vision* (Philadelphia: United Church Press, 1976), pp. 162–63.

20. Arthur Simon, *Bread For the World* (New York: Paulist Press, 1975), p. 5.

21. Clarence Jordan and Bill Lane Doulos, *Cotton Patch Parables of Liberation* (Scottdale, PA: Herald Press, 1976), pp. 109–111.

22. Jim Wallis, *Agenda for a Biblical People* (New York: Harper & Row, 1976), p. 18.

23. Karle Wilson Baker, "Pronouns," in *Worship Resources for the Christian Year,* Charles L. Wallis, ed. (New York: Harper & Bros., 1954), p. 401.

24. Shirley J. Hickman, ed., *Visions of Peace* (New York: Friendship Press, 1952), p. 4.

25. Peggy Billings, *Paradox and Promise in Human Rights* (New York: Friendship Press, 1979), p. 18.

26. Dieter T. Hessel, ed., *Beyond Survival: Bread and Justice in Christian Perspective* (New York: Friendship Press, 1977), p. 16.

27. Will D. Campbell, *Race and the Renewal of the Church* (Philadelphia: Westminster Press, 1962), pp. 23–25.

28. Paul Tillich, *The New Being* (New York: Charles Scribner's Sons, 1955), p. 10.

29. Jack A. Nelson, *Hunger for Justice* (Maryknoll, NY: Orbis Books, 1980), p. 4.